The South Coast

It is fitting our journey along the South Devon coast should begin at **Plymouth** as it is from these shores many great journeys have begun. Seafarers such as Drake, Raleigh, Hawkins, Frobisher, Cook, and of course the Pilgrim Fathers, all left from here to begin their epic voyages throughout the world.

The sea still plays an important part in the life of this bustling city, though its modern shopping centre and thriving night life prove to be equally popular attractions these days.

Plymouth, the largest city in the West Country, is situated at the mouth of two rivers – the River Plym and the River Tamar. The latter forms the boundary with Cornwall which can be reached by crossing the Tamar Bridge. The western part of the city is also home to Devonport Dockyard and the city's continental ferry port which offers daily sailings to French and Spanish shores.

It is the connections with Spain – and its infamous 16th-century Armada – which has given Plymouth lasting fame. Sir Francis Drake, though born several miles away near Tavistock, has been adopted by the city and is the name which appears most readily on the tourists' lips. His statue can be seen on the spacious Plymouth Hoe which offers superb views of Plymouth Sound – the area's main channel for boats. It was on the Hoe that Sir Francis insisted he should finish his game of bowls before sorting out the advancing Spaniards.

Drake's statue is not the only reminder of his existence. About a mile off the coast sits Drake's Island, once known as St Nicholas' Island, but changed in memory of the famous sea captain. It was once a fortress, but now encourages the invasion of tourists, who can catch a boat there during the summer.

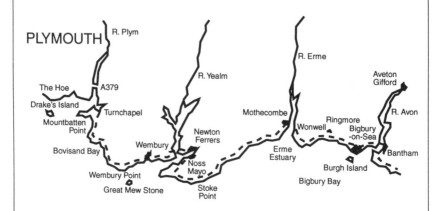

PLYMOUTH
R. Plym
R. Yealm
R. Erme
Aveton
Gifford
The Hoe
A379
R. Avon
Drake's Island
Turnchapel
Mothecombe
Ringmore
Bigbury
-on-Sea
Mountbatten
Point
Wonwell
Newton
Ferrers
Bovisand Bay
Wembury
Erme
Estuary
Bantham
Noss
Mayo
Burgh Island
Wembury Point
Stoke
Point
Bigbury Bay
Great Mew Stone

KEY

- - - - South Devon Coast Path

0   1   2   3   4   5
SCALE (Miles)

Explore the Coast of Devon

Paul Wreyford

Published by Sigma Leisure – an imprint of
Sigma Press, 1 South Oak Lane, Wilmslow, Cheshire SK9 6AR, England.

British Library Cataloguing in Publication Data
A CIP record for this book is available from the British Library.

ISBN: 1-85058-440-0

Typesetting and Design by: Sigma Press, Wilmslow, Cheshire.

Cover photograph: Teignmouth and The Ness at Shaldon (Paul Wreyford)

Maps: Mike Stonelake

Printed by: J.W. Arrowsmith Ltd, Bristol

This book is dedicated to Mum, Dad and Denise

Preface

Few counties in England can boast such a beautiful and diverse coastline as Devon. From the mild south with its popular seaside resorts to the rugged and spectacular scenery of the north, the coast of Devon has something for everyone. Superb sandy beaches, bracing cliff walks and charming fishing villages help attract thousands of visitors year after year.

Devon is the third largest county in England, though visitors are never more than 25 miles from the sea. Its thriving south coast has become one of the country's most popular holiday destinations. Torquay, where its famous palm trees line the promenade, is only beaten by Blackpool in the popularity stakes.

There are a variety of interesting places scattered all along the south coast, including historic maritime Plymouth; the tranquil riverside town of Dartmouth and the enchanting old world village of Branscombe.

The south coast is broken by a number of rivers and estuaries and is home to delightful secluded coves where smugglers once landed their goods. The distinctive red sandstone cliffs, to match the Devon soil, gradually turn to white chalk, and rise and fall to provide challenging walking and superb views of the English Channel.

Even more dramatic is the north coast, which is blessed with some of the most breathtaking scenery in the country. The boundless purple heather and yellow gorse cliffs of Exmoor contrast starkly to the harsh grey slate rocks of Hartland Point. Though there are fewer beaches in the north, the likes of Woolacombe and Saunton Sands are arguably among the best in the country.

This book aims to help those who wish to explore the coast of

Devon, whether it is by foot or by car. It is aimed at both the serious walker who may wish to complete the 180-plus miles, or the occasional rambler just wishing to take a stroll on a Sunday afternoon.

Every town, village and place of interest is featured as we follow the South West Peninsula Coast Path from Plymouth to Seaton, and from Lynton to Hartland.

The book also delves into the past to trace the area's varied history, covering stories of smugglers and wreckers operating on wind-lashed cliffs; tragic tales of ships wrecked on hazardous rocks and the many strange and eerie legends associated with the area.

I believe Devon has the most exciting and varied coastline of any county in England. Explore the coast of Devon for yourself and I am sure you will agree with me.

Paul Wreyford

Acknowledgments

My thanks to:

Chris Bryan, Chief Photographer of the Mid-Devon Advertiser, for his expertise and assistance

Mike Stonelake for the maps in this book

Mark Thornton for the camera

Liz Davey, Andy Pountain and Julian Mills for their company on many treks around the coast.

Contents

Introduction

Walking is a hobby more and more people are taking up. It is no longer just the 'mature' person who is enjoying the beautiful fresh air of the outdoors.

The South West Peninsula Coast Path is the longest in the country and one of the most beautiful. This book features the stretch along the south and north coast of Devon following the South Devon Coast Path and the Somerset and North Devon Coast Path. It does not pretend to cover every inch of the coastline. It only acts as a guide and to add interest to your walk. Walking is about exploring and seeing things for yourself – no book can be a substitute for the real thing.

Walking the coast of Devon should not be taken lightly. There are times when you may be miles from any town or shop, and climbs which leave even the fittest athlete panting.

It is not for me to tell you what to take with you when you go on a walk. Most people will have the common-sense to go prepared and know their limitations. However, I would strongly recommend an Ordnance Survey map. It is difficult to get lost on a coastal footpath – but not impossible. This book follows the most direct route along the coast, though there are diversions which are just as interesting. This is where a detailed map can be more than useful.

This book covers the cities, towns, villages and places of interest en route and gives you a brief account of what you can find there. Do bear in mind some attractions are only open during the summer months and vary their opening times.

Devon's coast is broken by a number of inlets and estuaries which means the distance of your walk could be doubled if the ferries are not running. There are tourist information centres at

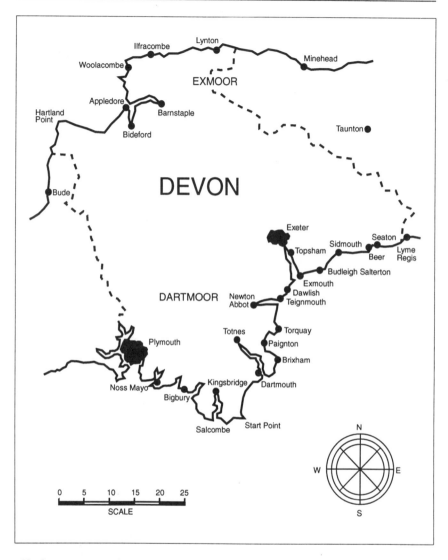

all the major resorts and towns where up-to-date ferry and tide information can be obtained.

A final warning is not to under-estimate the difficulty of your walk. One mile may be easy on a flat road, but Devon's coast is not flat. If it were, it would never be as interesting as it is!

The excellent view of the island and the many boats on the Sound can only be bettered by climbing Smeaton's Tower, which is a prominent landmark for both sailors and residents. The red-and-white-hooped lighthouse has sat at the very centre of the Hoe since the end of the 19th century when it was dismantled brick by brick from its previous location on Eddystone Rock.

Plymouth Hoe

A much newer attraction is the award winning Plymouth Dome. The popular visitor centre, opened as recent as 1989, gives people the chance to retrace the city's history through a number of modern displays. On the Hoe you will also find the imposing Royal Citadel. The enormous fortress was built by Charles II in 1666 to guard Sutton Harbour which sits below.

Sadly, much of Plymouth was destroyed by German bombs during the Second World War, though the harbour and its charming Elizabethan streets known as the Barbican escaped relatively unscathed. A walk through these narrow quayside alleyways, full of pubs and restaurants, will take you back into the past and it is easy to imagine rubbing shoulders with the country's leading seamen.

In the harbour you will find the Mayflower Steps, from which the Pilgrim Fathers boarded their ship to sail to the New World in 1620. The names of those hardy pioneers can be seen on a commemorative plaque on the quayside at Island House where they are believed to have lodged before setting sail. The harbour is still busy today, though most of the boats are trawlers filled with fishermen. These rusty, smelly working boats are contrasted by the yachts and cruisers sitting on the other side of the quay at Queen Anne's Battery.

The modern town centre is another reminder Plymouth is not still living in the past. As well as its excellent pedestrianised shopping centre it is home to the popular Theatre Royal which stages a number of top shows and plays throughout the year.

The South Devon Coast Path begins across the River Plym at **Turnchapel**. A frequent bus service covers the five-mile distance from the centre of Plymouth. Before heading along the path, you may like to make a little detour to Mountbatten Point to see the area where T.E. Lawrence, better known as Lawrence of Arabia, spent the latter years of his life. Lawrence was stationed here in the Flying Boat Squadron under the name of Shaw.

Slightly inland is Fort Stamford, just one of a number of fortifications in the area. It was built by Lord Palmerston in 1847 on the site of an ancient burial ground. It is now a popular leisure centre.

The path climbs over Jennycliff Bay and Staddon Heights towards the quay at **Bovisand** about a mile from Turnchapel. The harbour was originally built as an alternative to Plymouth Docks. From here you can take in the splendid view of Plymouth Sound for the final time. This is as close as you will get to the unusual Plymouth Breakwater which is an island sitting in the middle of Plymouth Sound. Above the quay is Fort Bovisand – one of the best preserved of the Palmerston forts.

The popular sandy beach at Bovisand Bay, which is backed by a number of caravans and chalets, is hidden around the corner and springs up on you quite unexpectedly. It is the first holiday centre on the South Devon Coast Path – but certainly not the last!

The walker has to pass straight through the caravan park to reach **Wembury Point** which is about a mile away. The view changes here and we now look south onto the vast English Channel. The imposing rock island directly ahead is the Great Mew Stone. The large population of gulls explains how it got its name as the word mew means gull. The seabirds once shared the island with a family who were banished to it by magistrates for seven years in 1744. It was also inhabited at the end of the 19th century by a man who bred rabbits for his landlord.

The point is also home to *HMS Cambridge* gunnery school. When the red danger flags are flying the footpath is closed due to firing and the walker is diverted inland.

Wembury Beach with St Werburgh's Church sitting above

Sitting about half-a-mile from the gunnery school is the village of **Wembury**. Most of the village is situated inland, though its most prominent building is a church which sits above Blackstone Rocks. St Werburgh's Church is named after a 7th-century saint and includes a 14th-century tower and Norman remnants. Wembury also has an interesting old mill, and was home to the descendents of Devon author John Galsworthy. The beach, with its excellent rock pools, is its most popular attraction.

About a mile-and-a-half along, the coast is broken by the Yealm Estuary. A ferry can be caught from Warren Point and will save the walker a ten-mile detour around the River Yealm. Unfortunately, it only operates on demand and so out-of-season walkers may have to catch a bus or be prepared for a long walk via the busy A379 road.

Boats on the shore at picturesque Noss Mayo

However you get across, two places which the visitor should not miss are **Newton Ferrers** and **Noss Mayo**, which sit opposite each other on the Newton creek of the estuary. The two villages are actually joined by a concrete path which can be used during low tide. Both are picture-postcard villages and popular during the summer. Old fishermen's cottages line the creek, while newer buildings sit on steep hillsides.

The narrow streets of Newton are well worth exploring and offer fine views of the river. The 14th-century parish church contains a nave which slants off to the right. It is believed to have been built this way because the head of Jesus, according to legend, fell to the right on the cross. The church across the river at Noss is a little newer, built during Victorian times. It was designed by Piers St Aubyn, whose ancestors once owned St Michael's Mount in Cornwall.

For the weary walkers who do venture around the estuary, a perfect stopping off place is the 16th-century Old Ship Inn at Noss Mayo. The historical pub, once a favourite haunt of smugglers, sits beside the harbour and offers excellent views of the estuary.

The path from Noss Mayo begins to follow a former carriage drive known as Nine Mile Drive. It was constructed at the end of the 19th century by Lord Revelstoke and circled his estate at Membland so he could show off the area to his distinguished visitors.

At Gara Point the coast faces the sea once more. Stoke Point, with its caravan park and sandy beach, is about two miles further along. Here you will find the ruined church of St Peter the Poor Fisherman. The 14th-century church was the former parish church of Noss Mayo, but was built almost two miles from the village. It is believed to have been built to double up as a guiding light to mariners which explains its strange position.

The path leads onto Beacon Hill and two miles towards the distinctive 30-foot high St Anchorite's Rock which is home to a number of seabirds. Once again, the coastline is interrupted a further two miles along – this time by the mouth of the River Erme at the aptly-named Mothecombe. There is no ferry, but the river can be waded at low tide.

The path on the eastern side of the River Erme can be picked up at Wonwell Beach. It leads to the impressive Beacon Point where the cliffs rise more than 300 feet above the sea giving superb views of Bigbury Bay now ahead of us. About a mile along is Hoist Point just above Westcombe Beach. It got its name from the days when locals hoisted seaweed from the beach to use as a fertiliser for their crops.

You may like to divert half-a-mile inland to **Ringmore** where you will find the Journey's End pub. Here R.C. Sherriff wrote his famous First World War play of the same name.

The main path continues for about half-a-mile to the horse-shoe-shaped cove of **Challaborough** where there is a sandy beach with a number of rock pools. It is a popular holiday centre as you will see from the number of chalets backing onto the beach.

The busy seaside resort of **Bigbury-on-Sea** is the heart of the bay and sits just around the corner from Challaborough. Tourists flock to its sandy beaches during the summer and also to see – and even visit – the impressive **Burgh Island** which sits a few hundred yards out to sea.

Crime writer Agatha Christie, a native of South Devon, is believed to have based her classic whodunnit 'Ten Little Niggers' (later renamed 'And Then There Were None') on the domineering island. In the book the island's visitors become stranded, though this should not be a problem at the real Burgh Island as it can be reached by a tidal causeway during low tide or via the resort's famous sea tractor which operates at high tide during the summer.

Not surprisingly many choose to stay on the island and reside at the elegant 1920s-style Burgh Island Hotel which dominates it. The island is also home to the 14th-century Pilchard Inn, which was another favourite smuggling post.

Isolated at the very top of the island are the remains of a stone building, once used as a summer house for picnics. Considering the panoramic view it affords, it is hardly surprising.

The coast path begins to travel north from Bigbury-on-Sea up along the River Avon – yet another interruption in the coast. At low tide the river can be waded, though extreme care should be taken. A seasonal ferry, if it is operating, will save a nine-mile round trip. There are riverside paths on both sides of the river to Aveton Gifford should you choose to walk around.

The destination across the river is **Bantham** which sits facing Burgh Island. It has a fine sandy beach which runs from the mouth of the river and is backed by the sand dunes of Bantham Ham. The village itself is yet another favourite haunt of smugglers and the 16th-century Sloop Inn was once owned by notorious smuggler and wrecker John Whiddon. The coast path continues over a golf course before skirting the inland village of **Thurlestone** which is located above a beautiful bay.

The weird Thurlestone Rock at South Milton Sands

The name Thurlestone comes from the Saxon word meaning 'pierced stone'. The explanation of this can be found on the popular sweeping beach of South Milton Sands where you will see the weird Thurlestone Rock complete with hole in it.

Sitting at the end of Bigbury Bay is Bolt Tail (the head is further along) with Hope Cove beneath it. The lovely **Hope Cove** is divided into two. In Inner Hope you will find delightful thatched cottages which have retained all the charm of this old fishing village, while at Outer Hope there is a small beach flanked by hotels.

Like most coves in the area it was popular among smugglers and can be reached by an authentic smugglers' lane. Hope Cove was also the scene of the only known English Shipwreck of a Spanish Galleon belonging to the Armada in 1588. Many of its relics have been found washed up on the beach over the years. Today, Hope Cove is more famed for its thriving shellfish trade and the local delicacy of crabs.

Hope Cove

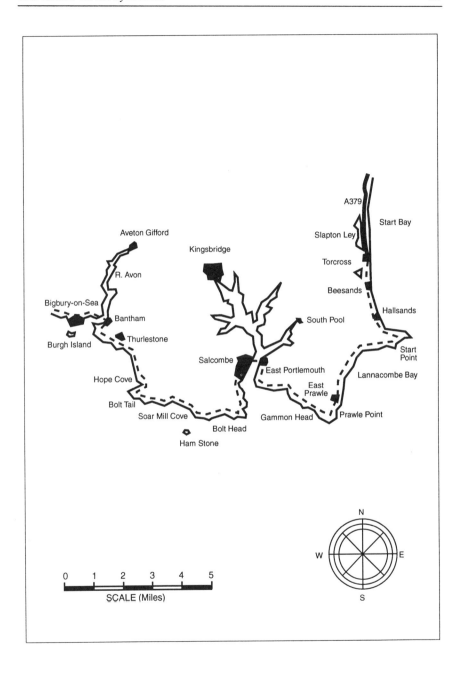

A379

Start Bay

Slapton Ley

Kingsbridge

Torcross

Aveton Gifford

Beesands

R. Avon

South Pool

Hallsands

Bigbury-on-Sea

Bantham

Start
Point

Burgh Island

Thurlestone

Salcombe

Lannacombe Bay

East Portlemouth

Hope Cove

East
Prawle

Bolt Tail

Soar Mill Cove

Gammon Head

Prawle Point

Bolt Head

Ham Stone

0 1 2 3 4 5

SCALE (Miles)

N

W E

S

The views from the wooded cliffs of Bolt Tail, which is about half-a-mile from Hope Cove, are spectacular and on a clear day stretch as far as the Lizard in Cornwall. The cliffs along to Bolt Head, about five miles away, are described by many as the most dangerous in Devon. Due to the crumbling cliff-face many rocks have formed weird and wonderful shapes over the years. They have also caused problems for ships and hundreds have been wrecked here.

From Bolt Tail the coast path climbs over Bolberry Down for about three miles before reaching Soar Mill Cove which is home to another sandy beach. Unlike many coves along this stretch of coast it can be reached via a footpath. Here you will also see Steeple Rock – one of the weird twisted pinnacles mentioned above. The large rock out at sea is Ham Stone.

Close to Bolt Head is a cavern called Bull's Hole into which a black bull supposedly entered and emerged a week later its coat completely white! From Bolt Head, the coast turns inland once more due to the Kingsbridge Estuary and heads towards Salcombe. About a mile along is **Sharpitor** where you will find the popular National Trust-owned Overbecks Museum and Gardens. Apart from the many exotic plants on display in the grounds there are excellent views of Salcombe Harbour and the popular South Sands beach directly below.

Beautiful **Salcombe** is the most southerly resort in Devon and a haven for yachtsmen. Its beautiful harbour and sloping streets attract thousands of visitors every year. Salcombe's position, sheltered from east and west winds, means it is blessed with one of the mildest climates in the country. Its palm trees and white-washed houses give it a Mediterranean feel.

The resort is best described as a sailor's paradise. On a summer's day the estuary is packed with boats despite an awkward bar at the entrance of the harbour to contend with. Lord Alfred Tennyson, a visitor to the town, is believed to have been inspired to write 'Crossing the Bar' after watching boats attempt to navigate the difficult passage into the harbour.

Boats in the quay at Kingsbridge

Salcombe is still a lively fishing community, though most of the boats which line the shore now belong to yachtsmen. A number of pleasure boats also leave from the harbour to take tourists up and down the river during the summer. The town was once an important shipbuilding centre and this era is heavily featured at the Overbecks Museum at Sharpitor. The Maritime and Local History Museum pays tribute to the RNLI and the many men who have risked, and sometimes lost their lives out at sea. A memorial at the attractive viewpoint area known as Cliff House Gardens was erected to honour those killed during the two wars, as well as the 13 who lost their lives during the tragic lifeboat disaster of 1916.

The parish church can be found on the summit of Church Hill and has a 15th-century pulpit and font. The chancel window is a memorial to the 11th Earl of Devon for his generosity in funding building work. The remains of Salcombe Castle, later renamed Fort Charles, is another popular attraction. It was built by Henry VIII and later became the last fortress in England to hold out for Charles I.

Most summer visitors head for the sandy beaches at North and South Sands or simply take a stroll around the many narrow streets. Whatever you choose to do in town, don't forget to try the local delicacy – Salcombe ice cream!

Sitting four miles inland at the head of the estuary is **Kingsbridge** – a pretty market town and capital of the South Hams. Most guide books will tell you the town gained its name from a bridge at the head of the tidal estuary which linked two royal estates in the 10th century. Most locals, however, will tell you the story of a Saxon king who needed to get across a brook called Dod. Because he could see no way of getting across, a young lad gallantly offered to get his feet wet and carry him on his back. The grateful King was so delighted he named the place 'King's Bridge'. Whatever story you wish to believe the town deserves some of your time.

The attractive quay, lined with yachts and glimmering fairy lights, is a beautiful starting point for a walk along the estuary.

The Kingsbridge Miniature Railway, a seven-and-a-half-inch gauge railway, runs trips along the quay for those wishing to let the train take the strain.

The old part of the town can be found up a steep hill known as Fore Street. Most of the shops here are modern, but the Shambles Arcade, built at the end of the 16th century on granite pillars, provides a nice contrast. Behind the arcade, which is now a restaurant, is the prominent St Edmund's Church which was built by the monks of Buckfast in the 13th century. Just outside you should look for the rather amusing epitaph of a contented 18th-century local. It reads:

'Here lie I at the chancel door, Here lie I because I am poor,
The further in the more you pay, Here lie I as warm as they.'

The town's most striking feature, which cannot fail to attract a passing eye, is its ball clock which sits proudly above the Victorian Town Hall. The clock was built with four sides, but with only three faces. The blank face pointed in the direction of the old workhouse and prevented the inhabitants counting time.

A visit to the Cookworthy Museum, named after Kingsbridge-born William Cookworthy who founded the china clay industry, is a must for historians. The museum, which was once the town's old Grammar School, is home to period costumes and many agricultural exhibits.

The rolling fields around Kingsbridge and its estuary are home to many old farm buildings – further evidence that agriculture, rather than tourism, was once the prime industry of the area.

On the eastern side of the estuary, sitting opposite Salcombe, is **East Portlemouth**, where the coast path begins once again. A ferry operates to and from its bigger neighbour across the water for those not wishing to travel via Kingsbridge. The village was once a busy port until the shipbuilders left for Salcombe. Ships frequently transported stone from nearby quarries.

The church of St Winwalloe is named after the saint who fled Wales in the 6th century. Its graveyard is home to many tombstones belonging to sailors – stark evidence of the rough coast we are soon to confront on our journey. Most visitors will find the sandy beach at Mill Bay a more appetising place to spend a few hours. It is as good as any beach on the other side of the estuary.

A mile walk across Portlemouth Down at the mouth of the estuary will take you to the Gara Rock Hotel from which the view along the coast is breathtaking. Jagged cliffs slope sharply towards the sea and provide the walker with superb coastal scenery. Gammon Head, about a mile further along, is no exception and is a favourite spot for photographers. It was also the scene of the most recent major shipwreck on the South Devon coast when the nine-and-a-half thousand-tonne cargo ship Demetrius broke its back during a Force 11 gale in December 1992.

The path continues for about a mile to **Prawle Point** – the most southerly-tip of Devon. The village of East Prawle is situated on the cliff above. The name Prawle comes from a Saxon word meaning 'to peep,' though the views from the headland deserve a longer look.

Many ships have been wrecked here, though the point was also the scene of a great British triumph in 1793 when the tiny *HMS Nymph* defeated the French warship *Cleopatra*.

A mile further along you will find the beaches of Lannacombe and Mattiscombe which are home to some strange earth pinnacles cut by the raging sea. The only protection for boats from the many twisted rocks along this stretch of coast, where five ships were wrecked in one night in 1891, is a lighthouse which sits at the very tip of the headland.

Start Point was once a wild and exposed area, but a car park and inland radio masts ensure the visitor is not too far from civilisation these days. Start Point Lighthouse is one of the oldest lighthouses in Devon and well worth a visit for its splendid views. It is from Start Point we get our first glimpse of Start Bay which stretches northwards and his home to many miles of beach.

One of those beaches can be found a mile away at the ruined village of **Hallsands**. The old village was tragically destroyed by a severe storm in 1917. At the end of the 19th century about 500,000 tonnes of shingle was removed from the beach to make concrete for the new docks at Devonport. It turned out to be a catastrophic error, for the beach level dropped by four metres leaving the village unprotected from the mighty sea. More than 30 houses were lost in the storm.

The remains of the houses can be seen on the beach and can be reached during low tide. They now sit as an eerie warning to those who dare to mess with nature. Not surprisingly, the new village was built a little further back from the sea!

The lesson was learnt a mile along at **Beesands** where huge boulders guard against a similar catastrophe. The tiny fishing village, with its famous Cricket Inn, is home to a distinctive triangular freshwater lake known as Widdicombe Ley. About a mile further along, the path drops to the delightful and unique village of Torcross.

Torcross and the long shingle beach of Slapton Sands

There can be very few places which boast a three-mile beach; a 270-acre freshwater lagoon and a Sherman tank in the visitors' car park! **Torcross** has all of these and much more. It has very few buildings, however, and most of these cater for tourists. The most unusually located are the row of cafes which sit virtually on the beach. All which separates them from the ocean is a new sea wall – something villagers wished they had in 1979 when a severe gale sent enormous waves literally crashing over the buildings.

The shingle beach which stretches beside the village is known as Slapton Sands. The road to Slapton runs behind it and is all which separates the beach from the freshwater lagoon belonging to **Slapton Ley Nature Reserve**. Naturalists and bird-lovers come from all over the country to seek out the variety of creatures which live among its reeds and marshes.

The village car park is close beside it and home to one of the more unusual monuments of the Second World War. The Sherman tank was fished out of the sea by a local innkeeper in 1984 and now stands as a memorial to 749 men who died during a training exercise which went tragically wrong. Slapton Sands was evacuated during the war so American troops could use the area to train for the D-Day Landings. In 1944, two training ships accidentally bumped into two German E-boats while training in the Channel. They were sunk and hundreds of bodies were washed ashore. It is believed the families of the dead were only told of the tragedy months afterwards – and then they were told the men had been killed in the real D-Day Landings at Normandy.

Another war memorial can be found on the beach at Slapton Sands, though this was erected as a thank you from the United States to all the evacuated residents. Fortunately, this beautiful area is now quiet and the only sounds come from reed warblers and lapping waves on the pebble beach.

The land rises again beyond Slapton and a road takes both the walker and motorist past Pilchard Cove to the tiny cliff-top village of Strete. The walker must then follow the A379 road out of the village towards Matthew's Point and Blackpool Sands a mile away.

Though it is nowhere near as big as its Lancashire namesake, **Blackpool Sands** is a popular spot for tourists. Its large sandy beach is sheltered by wooded cliffs and is another favourite haunt of windsurfers.

The road has to be followed inland again to reach the village of **Stoke Fleming** about half-a-mile away. The village church is well worth a visit if only to see the 14th-century brass of John Corp which is believed to be the oldest brass in the West Country. In the churchyard is the grave of child mathematician George Parker Bidder, known as the Calculating Boy. He became a top civil engineer and created London's Victoria Docks.

In the next mile-and-a-half, the coast path passes a number of secluded coves, before turning north as it reaches the mouth of the River Dart and the maritime town of Dartmouth. The picturesque town of **Dartmouth** is blessed with a proud naval tradition. Its narrow streets, full of tiered cottages, rise steeply from the harbour and offer superb views of the river.

The town was another popular area for smuggling and piracy during the Middle Ages and also had a thriving wine trade with Bordeaux. Geoffrey Chaucer's Shipmaster, who made his enemies walk the plank in 'Canterbury Tales,' came from Dartmouth and is believed to have been based on Medieval tycoon John Hawley.

At one stage Dartmouth was the county's principal port. In 1147, Richard the Lionheart assembled more than 2,000 men and 100 ships in the town to take on his crusade. Another 750 men in 31 ships left the same shores to help Edward III during his siege of Calais.

Gradually Plymouth became established as Devon's major port and Dartmouth was forced to take a back seat. During the battle with the Spanish Armada only two ships left from the town.

Sitting at the mouth of the Dart is Dartmouth Castle, which is strangely dwarfed by the 17th-century church of St Petrox which sits beside it. The castle was built by Henry VII during the late 15th century and still stands strong having survived a number of sieges.

About a mile along towards the town centre you will find another castle at Bayard's Cove. This fortress was built by Henry VIII, but little remains of it today. The cove is also home to the 18th-century Old Customs House where the Pilgrim Fathers moored for eight days in 1620 in an attempt to repair the damaged Speedwell. Television viewers may well recognise this particular area from the hit 70s' drama 'The Onedin Line' which was filmed here.

The strong naval ties are emphasised more strongly these days by the impressive red-brick building you will see towering above the town in the hills. This is the famous Britannia Royal Naval College where today's future seamen are put through their paces.

More seafaring escapades are captured in the town's Maritime Museum which is situated in the historical Butterwalk – a row of 17th-century houses now converted into shops.

Another place of interest is the Newcomen Engine House, which is situated in the Tourist Information Centre. It is named after Thomas Newcomen who invented the atmospheric beam engine. The museum contains an engine used down the Cornish tin mines during the 18th century.

Walking around Dartmouth, with its many steep hills, can be tiring. Because there is little room for cars many visitors choose to take to the water on one of the many pleasure boats which cruise up and down the estuary. A boat will take you three miles upstream to the small riverside village of Dittisham. On the opposite side of the bank, and partly-hidden on the hill behind trees, is **Greenway**, which became the luxurious home of Agatha Christie and is still owned by the family. It was also the birthplace of Sir Humphrey Gilbert who colonized Newfoundland in 1583. His half-brother was Sir Walter Raleigh, who was supposedly soaked by a Greenway servant with a bucket of water. The conscientious servant spotted the great man smoking tobacco and thought he was on fire!

Bayard's Cove, Dartmouth

The famous East Gate arch in Fore Street, Totnes

The River Dart, as the name suggests, runs all the way inland to Dartmoor. The first chance cars have of driving across is via a bridge at Totnes. The Elizabethan town of **Totnes** sits at the highest navigable point of the River Dart. It was once an important and busy port exporting tin and wool all over the world.

Totnes claims to be the second oldest borough in the country, having been established in the 10th century. The Brutus Stone which can be found embedded in the pavement in the sloping Fore Street marks the spot where Brutus landed in Britain and founded the British race, now named after him.

Most of the town's history can be found in the Elizabethan House which is home to Totnes Museum. Locals will also do their best to whisk you back into the past when they dress up in period costume every Tuesday during the summer. Fore Street is home to most of the town's shops. At the top of the street you will find the famous 15th-century East Gate arch spanning the narrow road.More history can be found in the 16th-century Guildhall which still used as a council meeting place as it has been for many years. The town's prison existed underneath the building until the 19th century.

The most prominent feature of Totnes is the ruin of the Norman castle which sits high above the town centre. It was built by Judhael, who commanded William the Conqueror's forces in the South West. At Steamer Quay on the eastern side of the river you will find Totnes Motor Museum which includes a collection of vintage cars and motorcycles.

There is a real laid-back feeling in Totnes and it is easy to think the locals barely raise a foot. But one person who did is commemorated on a granite obelisk outside the Royal Seven Stars Hotel. Totnesian William Wills and fellow explorer Burke became the first men to cross from the south to north of Australia in 1861. The mammoth expedition ended in tragedy, however, as both men died of starvation during the return journey. Wills was found with his open diary beside him. The Australians took the courageous explorers to their hearts and erected a monument outside Parliament House in Melbourne.

Another famous native was mathematician Charles Babbage whose original ideas of the 19th century inspired the invention of the calculator and computer.

Dartmouth Ferry taking motorists and walkers across the Dart to Kingswear

If the motorist does not wish to travel inland to Totnes, they can always join the walker and cross the River Dart via the Dartmouth Ferry, which is based close to Bayard's Cove. The short crossing is a delightful journey in itself. A small tug pulls a platform which can carry eight cars and a number of foot passengers. Be prepared for a long wait in the summer, however! The ferry's destination, a mere stone's throw across the river, is the village of **Kingswear**.

Though much smaller than Dartmouth there are a number of similarities. The most obvious is that both house a castle at the mouth of the river. Kingswear Castle was built by King John, but later rebuilt during the reign of Henry VIII. Unlike Dartmouth Castle it is privately owned. You will notice both castles sit exactly opposite each other. This was so a thick chain could be slung across the estuary mouth to prevent hostile ships entering. Kingswear is also the terminus for the Paignton and Dartmouth Steam Railway. From here you can take a trip through beautiful countryside to Paignton.

For those wishing to stick to the coast, a path will take you through a woodland area known as the Warren and to a number of coves which are hidden past the mouth of the estuary. These include Mill Bay and Newfoundland Cove. The latter is a re- minder of the thousands who left Dartmouth in the 16th and 17th centuries to begin a new life in the Newfoundland Fisheries of North America.

Slightly inland and accessible via a footpath is a day beacon known as the Daymark Tower which was a useful navigational aid for ships. At Inner Froward Point, the coast begins to swing round and head northwards. The walking can be tiring as the path winds up and down sloping gorse-clad cliffs. Above Pudcombe Cove is the National Trust-owned Coleton Fishacre gardens which are home to many rare plants and shrubs. The gardens were created by Lady Dorothy D'Oyly Carte of Gilbert and Sulli- van fame. The beautiful setting high on the cliff also offers superb views out to sea.

About a mile from Pudcombe Cove is Scabbacombe Head with Scabbacombe Sands beneath it. Another sand and shingle beach can be found at Man Sands a further mile along. From here the path continues for another mile to the distinctive Sharkham Point headland and the popular St Mary's Bay which sits around the corner beneath it. The wide, sandy beach can be reached via a steep footpath.

The main path continues to Berry Head Country Park which sits proudly above Brixham at the head of glorious Torbay, known to many as the English Riviera.

Beautiful **Berry Head** stands about a mile from the centre of Brixham. It offers us our first view of Torbay and even beyond to the East Devon and Dorset coast. In fact, 800 square miles of sea is visible from the 200-foot Berry Head cliffs. On a clear day the view extends as far as Portland Bill 42 miles in the distance.

Busy Brixham Harbour is dominated by a replica of The Golden Hind

The limestone cliffs are home to a number of rare plants, such as white rock rose and lilac sea lavender. The area is also a bird-watcher's paradise as the rugged cliffs attract a variety of seabirds including cliff-nesting kittiwakes, shags, fulmars and herring gulls. This particular stretch of coastline also boasts the south coast's largest breeding colony of guillemots – known locally as 'Brixham Penguins'.

As well as being an important natural site, Berry Head is also a notable historical spot. It was once home to an Iron Age fort, and more recently a Napoleonic fort which was built to protect the area from an attack across the Channel. The remains of the fort still stand – the only addition these days is a gift shop and cafe!

At the very tip of Berry Head is a lighthouse which is visible miles around. Because it is only 12 feet high and perched on a 200-foot cliff it has the distinction of being the country's shortest, but highest lighthouse!

The charming resort of **Brixham** is the least commercialised of the trio of towns which make up Torbay. Unlike its neighbours – Paignton and Torquay – it does not rely solely on the tourists for its livelihood. The fishing industry is still thriving, and Brixham Harbour is one of the busiest in the country. The town is built around the harbour, which echoes with the sound of ravenous gulls intent on sharing the day's catch – and your fish and chips if you let them!

Brixham has kept its old-fashioned charm and you are more likely to hear a Devonian accent at this end of the bay. Even so the town has still become one of the most popular resorts in the West Country and its narrow streets can become quite congested with traffic during the summer. Even the many trawlers in the harbour have to share the quay with a growing number of pleasure boats offering trips to the bright lights of Paignton and Torquay.

Though Brixham does have its popular Shoalstone and Breakwater beaches they are not large and so most visitors come to explore the town's many winding streets, which are filled with oak-beamed pubs and restaurants. One interesting building which never fails to attract a passing eye is the Ye Olde Coffin House, which as the name suggests, was built in the shape of a coffin! It was constructed by the lover of a local girl whose father had vowed he would rather see her in a coffin than married to him! Perhaps the father was tiggled by the man's sense of humour for he finally relented and allowed the couple to marry.

The town's biggest claim to fame is situated in the inner harbour. Here you will see the statue of William of Orange who landed in Brixham in 1688 on his way to the throne of England. Also gracing the inner harbour is a full-scale replica of Sir Francis Drake's The Golden Hind. Visitors can climb aboard to explore the tiny cabins and marvel at the collection of weapons and costumes from the period.

More treasures can be found in the town's museum, though you may prefer to look at some live ones on display in The Deep, which takes the visitor below the surface of the world's oceans.

Off the beaten track and not the most obvious tourist attraction is All Saints Church in Lower Brixham. The vicar of the church from 1823-47 was the popular hymn writer the Rev Henry Francis Lyte. When he was dying of tuberculosis he prayed for the inspiration to write something which would glorify God after he had gone. He presented 'Abide With Me' to his daughter three weeks before his death.

The coast path from Brixham takes the walker past a number of secluded coves situated within a wooded area. It skirts a golf course at Churston before heading to two popular beaches which can be found at Elberry Cove and the aptly-named Broadsands, about a mile-and-a-half from Brixham.

A steam train passes unnoticed at Broadsands

From Broadsands the path heads inland underneath a railway viaduct belonging to the Paignton and Dartmouth Steam Railway. It then turns towards Goodrington a mile away. A large caravan site, half-a-mile along, provides evidence you are coming to the heart of 'Grockle' country (tourists to those living outside the West Country!) The resort of **Goodrington** and its beach known as Goodrington Sands will tell you – if you had any doubt – you have arrived! With its sandy beach, two boating lakes, water flumes, and countless amusements it has no problem entertaining children and makes an ideal Torbay base for families.

A series of paths cut into the cliffs at the end of Goodrington Sands make a delightful evening walk as they are illuminated by colourful lights, similar to the famous Rock Walk at Torquay. A half-mile walk along the cliff will take you to Roundham Head and into Paignton which sits at the centre of the bay.

Paignton has become one of the country's leading seaside resorts, unashamedly promoting its long, sandy beach and bright lights of its many amusement arcades. It certainly does not live in the shadow of the even more popular Torquay and is a principal holiday centre in its own right. During the peak summer months the population of Paignton is almost doubled! Everything is geared towards the summer tourists; from its popular shows at the Festival Theatre on the Esplanade, to its famous old zoo on the Totnes Road. The 800-foot pier, with yet more amusements, is another favourite destination for families and is the longest pier in Devon.

The old part of the town, or what is left of it, nestles behind the many high street shops. The parish church built in Saxon times still remains, as does Coverdale Terrace which was part of a Medieval Palace belonging to the Bishops of Exeter. It is named after Bible translator Miles Coverdale who lodged here during Tudor times.

Paignton's grandest building is Oldway Mansion which sits slightly inland offering marvellous views from its beautiful grounds. It was built by Isaac Singer, best known for his sewing machines, in 1874. Linking its 100 plus rooms is an elaborate marble stairway and hall. Singer affectionately called the mansion his 'Wigwam,' though it was a little more expensive to construct and is believed to have cost in the region of £200,000! Paignton Urban Council paid a mere £42,000 for it in 1945 and turned it into municipal offices.

Oldway Mansion, Paignton

More charming relics from the past are preserved in the middle of the high street in the form of steam trains belonging to the Paignton and Dartmouth Steam Railway. Paignton is where the trains set off to journey through the countryside to Kingswear. The famous Flying Scotsman locomotive has been known to grace this stretch of track on occasions.

Unfortunately the three-mile train ride in the other direction to Torquay is a little more conventional, though the scenery is just as good. The railway track runs along the coast, and does so for much of the journey to Exeter, providing one of the most scenic railway journeys in the country.

The coast path to Torquay is sporadic, as it is all the way to Exeter, and the walker will have to frequently divert inland and follow the coast road.

After leaving Paignton, whichever way you choose to travel, you will pass more sandy beaches at Preston Sands and Holli-combe before arriving at Torquay – regarded by many as the jewel in the English Riviera's crown. There are very few people living in the south who have never visited, or wanted to visit, **Torquay** at some point in their lives.

Popular sunny beaches; spectacular night-time illuminations and of course its famous palm trees help make it one of the country's leading resorts. Thousands of tourists fill the hundreds of hotels and guest houses during the mass summer invasion.

The pace of life is slower in Cockington

Those who think Torquay is just a 'bucket and spade' resort usually change their minds after their first visit. Torquay offers a lot more away from the bright lights and crowded beaches. There are many parts of the town which have not been swallowed up by the commercialised world – and one of them is barely a mile away from the seafront. The turning to this little gem of the English Riviera is easily missed, as most have their eyes firmly set on the glorious bay when they approach the town centre from Paignton. The old-world village of **Cockington** is reached via a

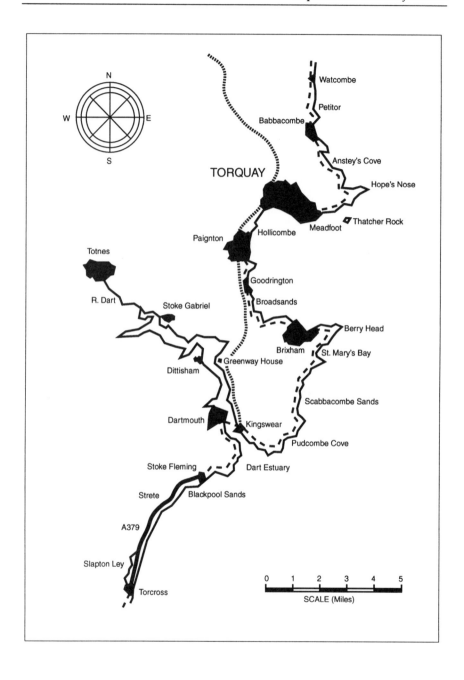

small country lane. In the summer you can travel to it in style via a horse-drawn carriage (did I say it was uncommercial?). It is almost as if time has stood still here and the bright lights of the town centre seem as far away as you can possibly imagine. The highlight of the village is its 14th-century forge where a black-smith can be viewed hard at work during the summer.

Back on Torquay seafront you can discover more of the area's history at Torre Abbey which sits facing the sea. The 12th-century monastery has a tithe barn in its grounds which held captured prisoners from the Spanish Armada.

Of course, all visitors are welcome today – though you might not be able to afford to stay in two of the bay's more expensive hotels. One of those is the prominent sea-facing Grand Hotel, where Torquay-born Agatha Christie honeymooned. The other, which sits at the far side of the bay, is the Imperial Hotel. Incidentally, don't bother looking for the original Fawlty Towers – the popular comedy series was actually filmed in Buckingham-shire!

Most of Torquay is built on hills and so walking can be tiring. One stroll worth taking is along the entwining paths on the illuminated cliff-face known as Rock Walk which backs onto the seafront. Up here you will be treated to some spectacular views of the bay. Princess Gardens is also tastefully illuminated during the evening and is home to the bay's second major theatre – The Princess Theatre. The Pavilions was once the town's major thea-tre, but has since been converted into a trendy indoor shopping precinct.

The Riviera Centre opposite Torre Abbey Sands is the unoffi-cial home of entertainment these days. It is a popular multi-en-tertainment complex complete with cinema and indoor swimming pool.

Torquay Marina and the adjacent harbour is, not surprisingly, jam-packed with boats of all shapes and sizes. The marina, full of luxurious cruisers, helps give the town a continental feel. Torquay has a number of beaches stretching along its coast. The coast path, which begins beside the Imperial, will take you to them. The largest is the sand and shingle beach at Meadfoot a mile away. It is popular during the summer as it can also be reached by road.

Palm trees flourish in popular Torquay

About half-a-mile inland at Wellswood, and well worth a visit, is Kent's Cavern – one of Europe's most important sites. The caves, which can be explored with the help of a guide, date back more than 450,000 years. Many of its prehistoric finds are on display at Torquay Museum in Babbacombe Road.

Back on the coast path you will soon enter the most exclusive part of Torquay – known locally as 'Tory Bay'. Out at sea is Thatcher Rock which is home to a number of sea birds. This is where locals will tell you there is hope after Thatcher – literally! Hope's Nose is a headland running gently down to the sea. It is popular among birdwatchers. The bigger rock out at sea is known as Ore Stone Rock.

More secluded beaches can be found within the next couple of miles at Anstey's Cove and Redgate Beach, though both are small and pebbled. A steep walk, via steps, from the latter will take you onto Walls Hill and to Babbacombe where you will be greeted with incomparable views of the remaining South Devon coast.

Babbacombe is a resort within a resort. It is quieter than Torquay, but has a number of sea-facing pubs and hotels. It also has the highest promenade in the country – the beaches of Babbacombe and Oddicombe sit nearly 300 feet below Babbacombe Downs!

The Cary Arms Inn, Babbacombe

Sitting on the sheltered Babbacombe Beach is the delightful Cary Arms Inn which recounts the unenviable story of Babbacombe's most famous son. It was in a house opposite the pub, now the beach car park, in which murderer John Lee carried out his grisly crime on his poor employer in 1884. It was not so much the murder which earned him lasting notoriety, but his execution –

or planned execution! For he became known as 'The Man They Couldn't Hang' after three failed attempts to administer justice. The Home Secretary changed the sentence to life imprisonment on humanitarian grounds. He was released in 1907 and died in America in 1933. Oddicombe Beach, which is larger than Babbacombe, is a stone's throw away. The less energetic will be pleased to know a cliff railway, linking the promenade and beach, operates during the summer.

Babbacombe will never rival its bigger neighbour on the opposite side of the bay, even though it does have its own theatre and a world-famous model village, but many say that is its appeal! Just around the corner from Babbacombe is Petitor, which is home to the bay's most secluded beach, being so far out of the reach of motorists. There are more secluded beaches further along the coast towards Shaldon which is about five miles away. This particular stretch of coast is known as the Roller Coaster, as the walker will no doubt testify. You have been warned!

The tiny village of **Watcombe** offers one of those small secluded beaches, as well as its own Valley of the Rocks which should not be confused with the more famous one at Lynton. The rocks were once mined for terra cotta clay. One distinctive inland rock is Giant Rock which was once a popular Victorian tourist attraction until it became obscured by trees which now make up this delightful woodland area.

Watcombe was also the place where engineer Isambard Kingdom Brunel chose to retire. Unfortunately he died before his mansion house had been completed.

The path continues through woodland to another small beach at Maidencombe less than a mile away. **Maidencombe** village is situated on a slope and is home to a number of delightful isolated thatched cottages. Author Rudyard Kipling lived in the village for a short time.

The beach is slightly larger than the one at Watcombe and can be reached by a car down the aptly-named Steep Hill which runs from the main coast road to Teignmouth. Motorists are treated to splendid views while driving along the B3199 road to Shaldon. To the east is the sea, while the west is home to open fields backed by the distinctive Haytor rocks on Dartmoor 15 miles away.

From Maidencombe, Shaldon is less than three miles away. Before the walker reaches it they must pass over Labrador Bay where 18th-century smuggler Captain Trapp built a cottage as a base for his illegal activities. Sadly, the cottage no longer exists. From here the path, and the road, drops once again and you will be treated to the beautiful sight of the Teign Estuary.

Shaldon sits on the beautiful Teign Estuary

The pretty Georgian village of **Shaldon** nestles at the mouth of the River Teign. A visit here is like stepping back into the past – especially if you arrive on a Wednesday in the summer when locals dress up in period costume. Shaldon's narrow streets are lined with modest Regency houses and charming village shops. There are also a number of places enticing the visitor to try a delicious Devonshire cream tea – few refuse!

Towering over the village is the imposing Ness Cliff which hides a delightful secluded beach. The only way to reach it during high tide is via an authentic smugglers' tunnel – but don't tell everyone! Ness Cliff is also home to the former Shaldon Zoo which became the Shaldon Wildlife Trust in 1985. Its collection includes a number of endangered mammals, reptiles and exotic birds. Sitting above the village are the colourful Botanical Gardens which offer superb views of the estuary.

A three-mile walk inland along the estuary will take you to the village of **Combeinteignhead** which is home to the delightful Coombe Cellars Inn. Smugglers once hid their contraband in the cellars of this beautiful riverside pub. Superb views of the estuary and its many fishing boats and wading birds can be enjoyed from the inn's large beer garden.

Three miles further along the estuary and sitting at its head is Newton Abbot – the capital of Teignbridge. At first sight, the busy market town of **Newton Abbot** seems to offer very little to encourage the visitor from the coast. Most people come here to visit its many high street shops or bring livestock to the popular weekly cattle market which has been running for more than 700 years. Others use it as a gateway to the coast, or to Dartmoor, as it is handily situated for both.

There are also plenty of interesting places to explore in the town itself. The most prominent and unusual building is the 60-foot St Leonard's Tower which stands yards from the town's pedestrianised shopping precinct. If it looks rather out of place it is because the tower once belonged to a church and is all that remains after the building was demolished in 1834. It was here the first declaration of William of Orange was read in 1688.

Another historical building is Forde House on the outskirts of the town. The beautiful mansion was built during the reign of James I and is now home to district council offices. The town is also home to a top racecourse where horses, greyhounds and even stock cars frequently compete.

The Teign Estuary can easily be crossed at Shaldon to avoid a long trip inland to Newton Abbot. At low tide it can be waded, though most foot passengers choose to join the motorists and cross via the Shaldon Bridge which has stood since 1827. Another alternative is to jump aboard the Shaldon Ferry which dates back to the reign of Elizabeth I.

The destination a few hundred yards across the estuary is the busy seaside resort of **Teignmouth**. Its long sandy beach is its main attraction and has been since Victorian times. The beach is dissected by the Grand Pier which marked the segregation point for male and female bathers during the 19th century. Today there are no such restrictions and the red-sanded beach is used to its full capacity on a summer's day.

Teignmouth viewed from Ness Cliff

Teignmouth has always been popular and has attracted many distinguished visitors. Because of its mild climate it became a popular 19th-century health resort. Among its residents was poet John Keats who lived in Northumberland Place for a short time in 1818. He came to tend to his brother Tom who was dying from consumption and had arrived in the hope the mild climate would save him. Unfortunately the weather was awful and the disillusioned poet left after three months. He did not depart without leaving his mark, however, and wrote many a sardonic remark about the area and its people.

Another early visitor was poet Winthrop Praed who, like Keats, also felt obliged to pen some words about the town – though his were a little more complimentary! Marine artist Thomas Luny obviously liked the place, for he built a house in Teign Street and lived there until his death in 1837. The house is now a hotel.

Bitton House, which is now occupied by the town council, was once the home of Sir Edward Pellew (Lord Exmouth). He gained national fame for leading the siege of Algiers in 1816 in which Christian slaves were liberated. More history can be found at Teignmouth Museum, which contains relics from a possible Armada wreck discovered off the coast in 1975.

Teignmouth is an active and pleasant resort which has no difficulty keeping the visitor amused. The grassy area adjacent to the seafront is known as the Den and a number of organised activities take place here in the summer. Apart from entertaining its visitors the town is home to a busy dock exporting ball clay all over Europe. Dartmoor granite was shipped out of the town and used to build London Bridge.

A footpath along the sea wall below Eastcliff will take you along the railway track for about a mile towards the Parson and Clerk headland at Holcombe. It does not reach neighbouring Dawlish, two miles away, so you will have to turn inland via Smugglers' Lane and join the road for part of the way. An alternative is to take the train and sit back and enjoy the splendid views out to sea. The odd and most striking feature about the resort of **Dawlish** is the railway track itself – as it literally runs straight through the beach! Bathers can step off the station platform straight into the sea!

• Dawlish is a delightful place to wile away the hours. Its long sandy beach is very popular and contains a number of coves to explore. The most popular is Coryton Cove where the rocks are often covered by a large population of mussels. A series of zig-zag paths in the cliffs lead to Lea Mount Gardens which are situated high above Coryton Cove. Here you can escape the crowds and enjoy fine views out to sea.

Most of the town centre is built around an attractive grassy area known as the Lawn. Running through it and out to sea is a brook which is home to a variety of waterfowl and the town's most famous inhabitants – its rare black swans. The swans originated from Australia and were a gift from Queen Victoria, who was a regular visitor to the town. Charles Dickens was another visitor and he used Dawlish as the literary birthplace of Nicholas Nickleby. Author Jane Austen was another who favoured the area.

About a mile-and-a-half along the sea wall and past a number of holiday centres and caravan parks is the remarkable **Dawlish Warren**. The two-mile sandy Warren acts as a natural bar to the Exe Estuary as its tip almost reaches Exmouth on the other side. Its golden beach, backed by sand dunes, is one of the best in the West Country.

At first glance, the Warren just looks like an extension of gift shops and amusement arcades, but it is an important nature reserve and popular all year round. Twitchers and nature lovers almost outnumber the hundreds of migrating birds which flock to its marshy shores. Guided walks and an information centre will help you identify the large variety of wildlife.

Wading birds and other forms of aquatic life can be found all along the estuary. Unfortunately the official coast path ends at Dawlish Warren and so those wishing to walk up the Exe must follow the road for much of the way. A seasonal ferry to cross the estuary to Exmouth can be boarded at Starcross two miles further along the coast.

Most people come to **Starcross** for the sole purpose of catching the ferry or to pass through on their way to Exeter. Though it is largely residential with a number of new homes and very few shops, Starcross is home to one very interesting building which sits alongside the railway line. Brunel's Atmospheric Pumping Station, now the headquarters of the local fishing and cruising club, was built in 1845 as part of the famous engineer's doomed Atmospheric Railway. The idea was for trains to operate using atmospheric pressure. The railway functioned through the use of a tube laid between the rails. Air was exhausted from the tube ahead of the train, which acted as a kind of vacuum and pushed the train onto the next station. The scheme was abandoned in 1849, largely due to miscalculations on Brunel's part. There were obviously other pumping stations in the area, but none remain as complete as the one at Starcross.

A flag flies high above Brunel's Atmospheric Pumping Station at Starcross

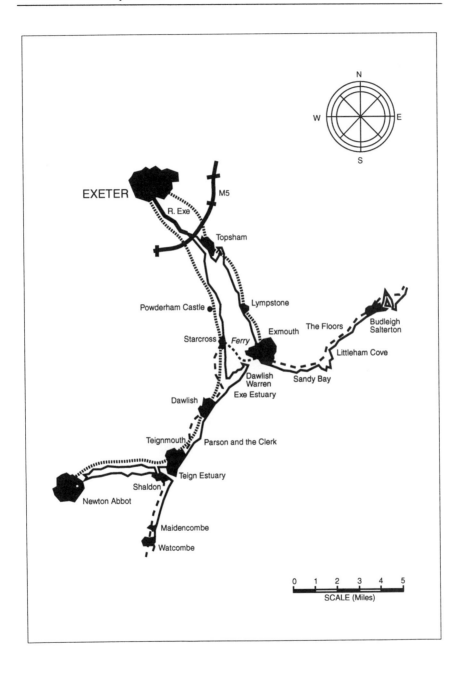

EXETER

M5

R. Exe

Topsham

Lympstone

Powderham Castle

The Floors

Budleigh
Salterton

Starcross   Ferry

Exmouth

Littleham Cove

Dawlish
Warren

Sandy Bay

Dawlish

Exe Estuary

Teignmouth

Parson and the Clerk

Teign Estuary

Shaldon

Newton Abbot

Maidencombe

Watcombe

N

W   E

S

0 1 2 3 4 5
SCALE (Miles)

Exeter Cathedral and its grounds provide a perfect place for shoppers to rest their weary feet

The adjoining coast road begins to cut inland at Starcross because of the grounds of the Medieval **Powderham Castle** – home of the Earl of Devon. The castle has belonged to the Courtenay family for more than 600 years. It was built between 1390 and 1420 by Sir Philip Courtenay. Apart from a number of magnificent State rooms, visitors come to walk around the spacious castle grounds which are occupied by an established herd of fallow deer.

The estuary begins to narrow past Starcross and eventually becomes the River Exe which runs through the city of Exeter about eight miles away. **Exeter** is the county town of Devon and one of the nicest cities in the country. It is smaller than Plymouth and its city centre is surprisingly compact with most of the places of interest within easy walking distance. The city was founded by the Romans nearly 2,000 years ago and is still surrounded by most of the wall they built during the 3rd century.

Like Plymouth, much of Exeter had to be rebuilt due to severe bombing during the Second World War, though a number of Medieval buildings can be seen sitting side-by-side modern shops and office blocks. Among them is the delightful Ship Inn, which was supposed to have been Sir Francis Drake's favourite watering hole.

There is no doubt Exeter's pride and joy is its 13th-century cathedral. Work on the impressive building was begun by Bishop William, the nephew of William the Conqueror, and took 90 years to finish. Beautiful stone carvings can be found on the walls, while inside is a memorial to R.D. Blackmore – author of the historical Exmoor romance 'Lorna Doone'. Sitting inside this grand building is awe-inspiring. You will appreciate the solitude and soon forget you are in the heart of a bustling city. Despite its size the cathedral is well-hidden behind many high street shops, and busy shoppers need not know it even exists. Another old building well worth a visit is the 14th-century Guildhall which is one of the oldest municipal offices in the country.

There is something around almost every corner in Exeter and it is easy to miss things. Parliament Street is no exception and you may have difficulty finding it, as it is reputed to be the world's narrowest street! Exeter, with such a vast history, is home to a number of museums as well as a ruined castle. The Rougemont Castle, built by William the Conqueror, received its name from the red sandstone from which it was built.

There is even something to see below the ground in the form of a maze of underground passages which was once part of a Medieval water supply. The entrance can be found in the Princesshay shopping precinct.

Out of the town centre, you may like to visit one of the country's top theatres. The modern Northcott Theatre can be found in the grounds of the city's university in Stocker Road.

It is easy to forget that Exeter was once a busy port or even has a river. A visit to the Quay will jog your memory. Here you will find the 17th-century Customs House and the world's largest collection of boats at the Maritime Museum, which sits at the head of the canal.

A mere four miles south of Exeter on the eastern side of the estuary lies the town of **Topsham**. Despite its close proximity to Exeter, it offers a welcome contrast to the hustle-and-bustle of city life and is therefore largely occupied by city workers who choose to live in a quieter environment.

Until the 19th-century the town was an important port on the River Exe, catering for the city's thriving woollen trade. It was the Romans who established it as a port, building a harbour and a road to link the town with Exeter when their ships were unable to get any further up the Exe.

Topsham prospered even further in 1290 when the Countess of Devon built a weir further up the Exe making it impassable to ships. The port became the city's only outlet to the sea until an Act of Parliament ordered the weir's destruction in 1539. Unfortunately the river had become unsuitable for navigation and so Exeter Canal had to be built in 1563 to overcome the problem. Topsham continued to survive as a port as there was now enough business for everyone. Ships built at Topsham even did battle against the Spanish Armada. It was the introduction of roads and the railway which finally made it redundant.

The town's past is reflected in many of its grand-looking buildings. On the Strand you will see elegant 18th-century Dutch-style houses which were built by merchant traders from Holland. Even the bricks which were used to build the houses were Dutch, brought back by ships which had carried exports. Many of the grand houses have high walls which hide delightful private courtyards and gardens.

Apart from its impressive houses, Topsham is home to a number of period pubs, some offering excellent views up the river. The main high street is also popular among visitors because of its many specialised shops. Because Topsham has so many historic buildings, the whole town is now a conservation area!

The railway track from Exeter runs all the way to Exmouth and at the village of **Lympstone**, four miles from Topsham, is carried high above the houses on tall viaducts.

Lympstone Village, with its narrow lanes, is smaller and quieter than Topsham. Its most prominent building is the clock tower in the harbour known as Peter Tower. The red-bricked tower was built in 1885 by W.H. Peters in memory of his wife Mary Jane who was devoted to helping the poor people of the village. The small quay is also home to a number of boats and a popular sailing club.

The centre of Exmouth is only about two miles from here and can be reached by a riverside path. The busy resort of **Exmouth**, as the name suggests, sits at the mouth of the Exe Estuary. It is Devon's oldest seaside resort and especially popular among families because of its two miles of golden sand.

The town became popular as a resort in the mid-18th century when residents from Exeter came in the belief the sea would benefit their health. Its fame was advanced by local resident Sir John Colleton who brought the first ever Magnolia tree to British shores from South Carolina. It was known as a 'giant tulip' in those days and can be seen in various forms throughout the town.

Exmouth offers visitors all the expected holiday attractions including a popular model village on the seafront known as The Wonderful World of Miniature where you will find the world's largest 00 scale Model Railway complex.

The Pavilion at the centre of the Esplanade is the town's unofficial entertainment centre hosting concerts, dances and local amateur dramatics. Exmouth Fun Park, with its boating lakes and bouncy castles, is a more favoured destination among children.

The town is home to a number of interesting buildings. The Beacon, a row of delightful Georgian houses overlooking the seafront, is where Lady Byron and Lady Nelson once resided. Exmouth also has some unusual buildings. None more so than the circular 18th-century A La Ronde which can be found two miles north of the town in Summer Lane. To be exact the house is not totally round as it has 16 sides. Its tiny rooms are lit by a lantern which sits in a gallery decorated by shells. It is now owned by the National Trust and well worth a visit. A little further up the lane you will find the aptly-named Point-in-View Church. The building is not so unusual, but its location so far away from civilisation is. It was actually built by two wealthy cousins who found it difficult to journey into town every Sunday and so had the chapel built on their own 15 acres! It also doubled up as a small school with accommodation provided in the few alms-houses which were built around it.

Like many seaside resorts Exmouth was once a busy port and was used as a base by Sir Walter Raleigh. The docks, hidden to the west of the town, are still busy today. Because of its excellent beach, it is a popular base for a number of watersports, such as water skiing, sailing and windsurfing. The two-mile beach stretches to Orcombe Point. Another long stretch of sand, known appropriately as Sandy Bay, can be found just around the corner. Sandy Bay is home to an enormous caravan park and the Country Life museum, which has a deer park and vintage cars among its attractions.

The coast path, which begins at the Foxholes Cafe, passes the many caravans at Sandy Bay and over Littleham Cove – a sand and shingle beach well used by the bay's many inhabitants. It peaks at a height of about 400 feet at The Floors before skirting the boundary of a golf course and dropping to the unspoilt resort of Budleigh Salterton, five miles from Exmouth.

Though it was scarcely recognised as a resort until Edwardian times, **Budleigh Salterton** has had more than its fair share of important visitors and residents. Its most famous was Sir Walter Raleigh who was born at nearby Hayes Barton, East Budleigh, in 1552. The Tudor farmhouse can be viewed from the road and is occasionally open to the public.

Artist John Millais painted his classic 'Boyhood of Raleigh' on the three-mile pebble beach at Budleigh Salterton. The resort was also made famous by literary giants such as Noel Coward and P.G. Wodehouse. Anthony Trollope was another who lived in the village for a short time.

The resort got its strange name from the long-abandoned salt-pans which were once worked at the mouth of the adjacent River Otter. The splendid and distinctive wood of beech trees on the adjoining cliff is a popular local landmark and is visible from miles around.

Budleigh Salterton is a quiet and elegant resort with a high street full of unusual and privately-owned shops. In the town centre you might like to visit The Fairlynch Museum which is an 18th-century thatched cottage containing period costumes and a display of model ships.

Bicton Park, designed by the same man who created the gardens in the Palace of Versailles, consists of 50 acres of gardens and can be found two miles inland. Another attraction close by is Otterton Mill which is fed by the River Otter. It is one of the few surviving watermills left in the country and open to the public as a museum.

The River Otter can be crossed via a bridge less than half-a-mile upstream. The path runs for three miles to Ladram Bay where the red sandstone cliffs rise to 500 feet. The sandy beach comes complete with caves and a number of sandstone pinnacles including the prominent Big Picket Rock which sits slightly offshore. The path runs through woodland and up onto High Peak before slowly descending towards Sidmouth about a mile away.

Quiet Budleigh Salterton

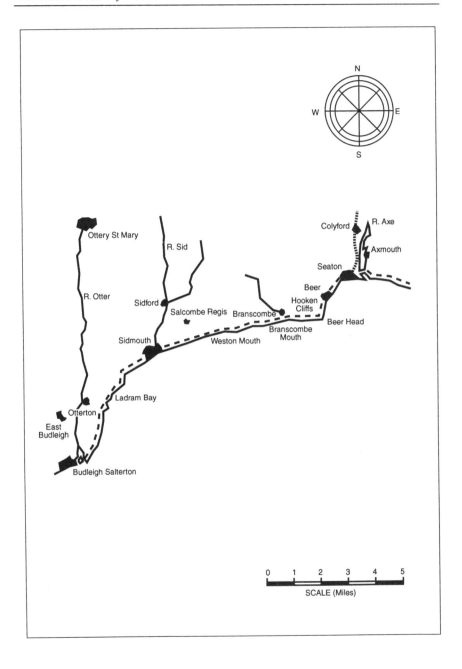

The geriatric capital of Devon is not an unfair label to attach to **Sidmouth**. It is not surprising the elderly choose to settle on its placid shores for it is one of the loveliest and least commercialised resorts in the county. Of course, Sidmouth contains the usual seaside trimmings, but the pace of life is evidently much slower. The town's elegant buildings also give it a certain grace which other resorts often lack. This elegance is reflected in the Regency architecture which is evident all around the town.

Like Budleigh Salterton, Sidmouth has had its fair share of distinguished visitors. The Grand Duchess Helen of Russia once stayed in Fortfield Terrace which overlooks the town's cricket pitch. The Duke and Duchess of Kent also stayed in the town with their daughter Princess Victoria in 1819. They resided at Wool-brook Cottage which can now be seen as the miniature Gothic castle The Royal Glen Hotel. The town's church contains a memorial window to the Duke of Kent who died in Woolbrook Cottage a few months after arriving there. More of the town's history can be found in Sidmouth Museum in Church Street. Regency prints and Victorian costumes are among the many items on display.

Those who think Sidmouth caters just for the elderly would be wrong. Children – and adults – will love the Vintage Toy and Train Museum in the Market Place which is home to a number of period toys. In August every year, the town bursts uncharacteristically into life when it plays host to an international folk festival.

The one mile-long pebble beach is not surprisingly the town's biggest draw. Jacob's Ladder with its many rockpools to the west of the resort is also extremely popular. So is Connaught Gardens which sits above and offers beautiful sheltered walks with excellent views back along the coast to Berry Head.

Sidmouth sits on the River Sid between two sloping red cliffs. To the east is the beautiful Salcombe Hill which comes tumbling down to meet the town. From here the coast path can be rejoined, though you may like to divert two miles inland to the tiny village of Sidford, famous for its 16th-century Porch House. This is where Charles II is thought to have sheltered following his narrow escape from Cromwell's men at Charmouth during the Civil War. The village also has a sanctuary for retired donkeys which is open to the public.

Branscombe has a popular beach and wonderful cliff walks

The path at Salcombe Hill climbs steeply to about 500 feet, before dropping past the village of Salcombe Regis which sits half-a-mile inland. **Salcombe Regis** is older than Sidmouth and a manor of King Alfred – hence the suffix. The prefix comes from the monks of Exeter who worked the salt pans at the mouth of the combe. The most prominent building in the small village is the 12th-century church of St Peter. The tower was frequently used to store smuggled goods.

The coast path passes over Dunscombe Cliff where it once again rises to 500 feet above the sea. At Weston Mouth, which is about two miles from Sidmouth, there is a long shingle beach which is never too crowded because of its remote position.

The coast path continues for about two miles until it is dis- sected by the gorgeous village of **Branscombe**. The shingle beach at Branscombe Mouth is dominated by the Sea Shanty Cafe which was once a coal yard. The actual village – one of the longest in Devon – is spread inland along a beautiful valley. Its pretty thatched cottages help make it one of the most picturesque and best-preserved places in the county.

The tiny fishing village also belonged to King Alfred during the 9th century, but like Salcombe Regis, soon found its way into the hands of the Benedictine Monks of Exeter.

The Branscombe family lived at Edge Barton on the hillside until the 14th century. Walter Branscombe became Bishop of Exeter in 1258 and was involved in the building of the city's cathedral. There is plenty of history on show in the village including a Tudor forge and an ancient bakery where the ovens are still fired by faggots.

The village church dedicated to St Winifred is well worth a visit. It has a three-decker pulpit and a priest's room located in its Norman tower, which is just one of a dozen or so still surviving in England.

On leaving Branscombe the coast path begins to climb East Cliff. The walker is soon faced with the choice of following a path up along Hooken Cliffs or following the official route below.

Hooken Cliffs are famous for a dramatic landslide in 1790 when about ten acres were lost.

About a mile along is the jutting Beer Head where the views extend to Start Point on a clear day. No doubt you will have noticed the red sandstone cliffs have now been replaced by cliffs of chalk. These are reputed to be the most westerly in Britain. The path heads northwards and drops past a caravan site to the charming resort of Beer, about a mile away.

The white cliffs of Beer

It is sometimes difficult to believe the peaceful fishing village of **Beer** was once the centre of Devon's smuggling industry. It was also home to the county's most celebrated smuggler – John Rattenbury. A walk along the pebble beach at low tide will reveal a number of nooks and crannies where smugglers may have secretly landed and stored their booty.

If it's exploring you enjoy then a visit to Beer Quarry Caves, which offers guided tours of its network of underground caverns, is a must. The Romans were the first to dig the quarries for building stone nearly 2,000 years ago. Part of Exeter Cathedral was built using Beer stone. Lace-making was another thriving industry and Beer is believed to have provided £1,000 worth of trimmings for Queen Victoria's wedding dress. Fishing is the main occupation today and you may catch a glimpse of the fishermen still using old capstans to haul their boats from the water.

The main street, with a number of fascinating local shops, slopes gently down to the harbour and has a narrow brook trickling beside it. At the parish church you will find a memorial to a victim of the plague which swamped this tiny village in 1665. Children may be more interested in the Pecorama Pleasure Park, however, where there are a number of model railway layouts set in luscious grounds. Fine views across the bay can be obtained from Jubilee Gardens, which sits above the beach.

The mile-long pebble beach at Seaton

The larger resort of Seaton can be found around the next headland known as White Cliff, for obvious reasons. **Seaton** is a busy holiday resort backed by the lush green hills of the Axe Valley. It is full of caravan sites and guest houses and caters solely for the holidaymakers who flock to its one mile-long pebble beach.

Seaton Hole to the west of the resort contains a number of rock pools and is a particular favourite haunt of children. The town centre is home to the usual seaside attractions, but also has some beautiful gardens. The resort's most famous attraction is the Seaton Electric Tramway which was built on a disused railway and runs alongside the River Axe to Colyford and the historic town of Colyton. The narrow-gauge open top cars are the last of their kind in the country.

Boats moored at the mouth of the Axe

The River Axe is another favourite spot for 'twitchers' as it is home to a number of species of wading birds. Sitting inland on the other side of the estuary is **Axmouth** which was once a popular working port during the Middle Ages. Evidence is provided by the Great Ridgeway – a prehistoric track which runs from here through Dorset and as far as East Anglia and the Wash. As recent as 1825 engineer Thomas Telford considered constructing a canal from Axmouth to Bristol to save ships having to journey around Lands End. A copper bolt in the wall of the Norman church marks one of the survey stations. The Axe is crossed via the Axe Bridge which was built in 1877 and believed to be one of the earliest concrete bridges in the world.

The coast path cuts inland through a golf course, but soon returns to the cliff edge and runs through an area famed for its landslides. The most dramatic occurred on Christmas Day in 1839 when eight million tonnes of rock and earth belonging to Downland Cliffs plunged into the sea taking many houses with it. The area is now an important nature reserve as the trees and plants have grown without human interference. Naturalists have sighted more than 100 different species of birds, including the rare nightingale.

The Devon-Dorset border can be marked by Chimney Rock – a sandstone pinnacle below the village of **Ware** which sits about four miles from Seaton. Lyme Regis is a mile further along.

The North Coast of Devon

We begin our journey along the north coast within the boundaries of beautiful Exmoor.

The Somerset-Devon border is marked by **County Gate** on the A39 road which is about a mile from the coast. It was said the gatekeeper used to sleep with his head in one county and his feet in the other! There is a car park and tourist information centre here, making it an ideal starting point. A footpath takes the walker to the coast at Glenthorne where the official Somerset and North Devon Coast Path can be joined. The main path hugs the coast closely and skirts the 1,135-foot Old Barrow Hill which is home to the remains of a circular Roman signal station.

The tree-covered island a little further along sitting out at sea is known as Sir Robert's Chair. It was named after Sir Robert Chichester who was shot and killed near Lynton. Locals were once so convinced his ghost drove a flaming coach along the cliff at night, they hired the rector of Bratton Fleming to exorcise the spirit. It is not known whether the rector was successful!

The path runs along the cliffs above Countisbury Cove for about three miles to the distinctive headland known as **Foreland Point**, which is the most northerly point of Devon. The 50-foot lighthouse on its tip is reached via a private road. Around the corner of the headland you will see Sillery Sands, a secluded beach which can be reached via a long, steep path. It is a popular destination for boats leaving from the shores of Lynmouth which is less than two miles from here.

Inland is the village of **Countisbury** and its famous hill which is believed to be where King Alfred defeated the Danes in 878. The name comes from a Celtic translation of 'the camp on the headland,' though many see it as a corruption of 'county's boundary' because of its position so close to the border.

BRISTOL CHANNEL

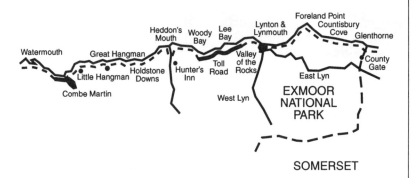

KEY

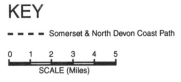

- - - - Somerset & North Devon Coast Path

0   1   2   3   4   5

SCALE (Miles)

The path crosses Wind Hill about a mile away, before dropping towards Lynmouth. An alternative route also begins from the village, going inland and following the beautiful East Lyn River.

Charming Lynmouth can be full of tourists on a summer's day

The twin resorts of **Lynton** and **Lynmouth** are a mere 600 feet apart . . . vertically! Lynton sits on the cliff-edge offering superb views of the rugged coastline, while its sister nestles beneath, tucked away at the bottom of a steep wooded gorge.

It is not surprising visitors flock to these charming resorts as they combine to make this one of the prettiest areas in Devon. Because they sit isolated in the wilderness of Exmoor they receive more than their fair share of visitors, though this should not put you off becoming one of them.

Lynmouth is the more popular of the two villages, sitting at the mouth of the River Lyn. The resort, though small, can well accommodate its many visitors as it has a number of hotels and guest houses lining the riverside. Many literary greats have stayed on its placid shores. The most famous is the poet Percy Shelley – though he was certainly not welcomed with open arms! He came with his 16-year-old bride Harriet Westbrook to escape from her furious parents. They stayed for just nine weeks. It was Shelley's custom to write propaganda tracts and cast them out to sea in bottles. One of these leaflets, entitled 'Declaration of Rights,' was deemed a little too seditious and the authorities ordered his arrest. He escaped to Wales in a rowing boat with the help of a local. Shelley's Cottage was destroyed by fire in 1907, but later rebuilt and renamed Shelley's Hotel. It can be found opposite St John's Church.

Lynmouth's idyllic location has also led to its downfall. In 1952, after weeks of rain, the East Lyn River burst its banks bringing down tons of earth, trees and boulders. Thirty four people lost their lives as they were swept out to sea along with many of the resort's buildings. The severity of the flood is highlighted by a mark on a cottage which shows the height the floodwater reached. Nine inches of rain is believed to have fallen in one night. Few buildings survived the tragedy – the most notable being the pre-Victorian Rock House.

One prominent feature of the village is the Rhenish Tower which sits on the jetty. The tower, which is still used as a beacon for local fishermen and sailors, is believed to be an imitation of a Rhineland tower. It also had to be rebuilt as the original was destroyed in the flood.

The two villages are linked by the main Lynmouth road, though the energetic may like to reach the top using the twisting footpath on Lynmouth Hill. The other alternative is to travel via the cliff railway which operates by the waters of a cliff-top stream. When it was first built in 1890 its one-in-four climb was believed to be the steepest gradient of any railway in the world.

Lynton has also had its share of distinguished visitors, including Wordsworth and Coleridge. Visitors were once few and far between because of the terrible roads across the moor. In the late 19th century publisher Sir George Newnes established the area on the tourist map by creating the Barnstaple-Lynton Railway.

A cliff railway links the resorts of Lynmouth and Lynton

It only stayed open until 1935, but by then the roads had improved and Lynton had become a popular resort. The former railway is heavily featured at the Lyn and Exmoor Museum which is housed in a 16th-century cottage. Newnes also built Lynton Town Hall – as a 21st birthday present for his son!

If its excellent views you are after then a climb up Summer-house Hill is a must. From the top you will be treated to outstanding views out to sea and inland across the wilderness of Exmoor. The most popular attraction lies just west of the resort and can be reached via the road or by the coast path over Hollerday Hill.

The spectacular **Valley Of The Rocks** consists of a number of steep hills capped with huge granite rocks and littered with fragments of stone. This magnificent rocky valley is believed to have been formed during the Ice Age 10,000 years ago. The impressive Castle Rock, which guards the valley entrance, can be reached via some stone steps which take you 800 feet above sea level. In the 19th century an old hermit woman named Aggie Norman lived here and became the inspiration for Mother Melldrum in R.D. Blackmore's classic 'Lorna Doone'. Mountain goats still live in the valley and can be seen precariously perched on the rocks.

At dusk the valley can be quite eerie and it is easy to let your imagination run riot. If you stand and face Castle Rock from the Lee Abbey road, which runs through the valley, you will see the White Lady. She is formed by the sky which is visible through a gap in the rocks. Wringcliff Bay, which has a mixture of sand and shingle, can be reached via a path from here.

The cliffs between Lynton and Combe Martin are a rock climber's dream. At points they reach more than 1,000 feet and are among the highest in the West Country. Walkers should be warned this is one of the toughest sections on the coast path.

Upon leaving the Valley of the Rocks the walker has to join the motorist on the Lee Abbey road as the coastline at Duty Point falls on private property. On the Point you will see a tower once occupied by duty coastguards on the look-out for smugglers – hence the name.

The 19th-century **Lee Abbey** sits on a toll road. Its name is slightly misleading as it was built as a private residence and not as a church. It was built on the site once occupied by the former squires of Lynton, known as the Whichehalses – another familiar name from the pages of 'Lorna Doone'. It is now used as a Christian conference centre. Lee Bay is another area famed for dramatic landslips. The beach is accessible but bathers should be aware of strong currents and fast tides.

The road continues through a woodland area known as **Woody Bay** which is home to a rushing torrent and the Crimean Inkerman Bridge. The oakland woods, which stretch for nearly two miles, perch high on the cliff and roll down to the sheltered bay which is home to a sand and shingle beach. On emerging from the wood, the path passes the site of a 1st-century Roman fort which was built to keep watch for potential attacks from the Welsh.

About half-a-mile further along, below the distinctive Highveer Point, is the dramatic **Heddon's Mouth** – a gorge which sits between 800-foot hills. There is a sand and shingle beach here as well as the ruins of an 18th-century kiln which once burnt limestone.

The River Heddon itself runs inland and is banked by two paths on either side which make a delightful two-mile-round walk to the Hunter's Inn, should you be seeking refreshment. The Inn, which is set in a delightful woodland area, can also be reached by a narrow lane off the A39. It is a favourite base for fisherman who come to try their luck on the clear waters of the river.

The coast path crosses the river on a small bridge about half-a-mile inland for those not wishing to walk as far as the inn. The climb up the other side is very tiring and not for those with a fear of heights. Needless to say the view back along the valley is spectacular.

The path then crosses the beautiful hills of Holdstone Down which reach more than 1,000 feet in places. This part of the coastline is home to many secluded beaches but most are only accessible to the experienced climber.

The beautiful waterfall at Sherrycombe, three miles from Heddon's Mouth, tumbles over the cliff and is crossed by the walker at its head. Unfortunately it needs to be viewed from the sea to appreciate its full beauty. A Boat trip from Lynmouth or Combe Martin will provide the simple solution.

By now you will no doubt have noticed the daunting obstacle less than a mile ahead. Yes, you will have to walk up it! The forbidding **Great Hangman**, a 1,043-foot hill, rises at 45 degrees. Because of the angle, the climb should be treated with caution, especially when the ground is wet. Not surprisingly the views from the summit – which is the highest point on the South West Peninsula Coast Path – are unrivalled.

The walker will be pleased to know its downhill most of the way to the less intimidating 716-foot Little Hangman a mile away. It overlooks a beach known as The Rawns – once a popular spot to find edible seaweed known as laver. Little Hangman hill is reputed to be where a sheep thief accidentally hanged himself when a rope attached to one of his flock became caught around his neck!

The larger and more accessible shore on the other side of the hill is Wild Pear Beach which is reached via a steep path. The main footpath leads to Combe Martin Bay, less than a mile away. It is here we leave Exmoor National Park behind us.

The delightful resort of **Combe Martin** lies at the bottom of a valley and offers a comforting break from the desolate coastline. Its two-mile main street, full of gift shops and small hotels, is reputed to be the longest village street in the country.

Combe Martin's popular beach known as Sandy Bay is a little deceiving as it is mostly made up of shingle and a number of rocks. The village was once home to an important industry. Mining for silver began here during the reign of Edward I. It is believed silver from Combe Martin helped pay the cost of wars with France during the reign of Edward III and Henry V. Today, the village is more famous for its strawberries and other fruits which form a thriving local industry.

The resort's most prominent building is the parish church of St Peter which has a 12th-century tower rising more than 100 feet. It is well worth a visit as it contains a number of interesting features. Combe Martin is also home to a popular motorcycle museum containing more than 50 British models.

The resort's most unusual building is The Pack O' Cards inn which was built in the 18th century by lucky gambler George Ley from his winnings. To celebrate his success he built it with four floors; 13 doors and 52 windows – one for each card in the pack!

The coast path leaves Combe Martin beside the A399 road for about half-a-mile before heading back along the coast. It passes the edge of Bamant's Wood and a caravan site before reaching Small Mouth where there is another beach with a number of caves to explore. The path then crosses the head of an inlet which is home to an impressive 19th-century Gothic castle.

Watermouth Castle was built as recent as 1825. Today, it has been transformed into a mini-theme park. Among its attractions are a smugglers' dungeon, a maze and children's fun fair rides. It is also home to some beautiful terraced gardens and delightful woodland walks. At Watermouth Cove you will find a thriving boating centre. Pleasure boats will take you around the many coves which can also be explored on foot during low tide. During low tide you can follow the path along the foreshore. Otherwise the walker must follow the road for a short distance before rejoining it. Both routes are clearly signposted.

From Watermouth, the path rises to Widmouth Head about a mile away. As it rises you will be treated to superb views of the inlet and Great Hangman to the east. It then turns south into Samson's Bay. Hele Bay, three miles from Combe Martin, is just around the corner.

The village of **Hele** is home to a grand 16th-century watermill responsible for producing flour. Its bay has a safe shingle beach which is popular among canoeists. There are also a few amusements and a tide-filled children's swimming pool.

Watermouth Castle

From Hele the path climbs up and over the impressive 447-foot Hillsborough hill. Its summit is one of the few places in the country where you can stand and watch the sun rise and set over a sea horizon. It also provides us with our first good view of Ilfracombe Harbour.

The busy resort of **Ilfracombe** nestles between towering green hills. It is another welcome sight on this remote and sometimes harsh, wind-swept north coast. It is not difficult to understand why Ilfracombe has become North Devon's most popular holiday destination. All the usual seaside attractions can be found here, including the famous Pavilion Theatre where top name stars tread the boards.

Of course, most people come to the seaside for the beach – and there are enough of those in Ilfracombe. Unfortunately most lack good sand and are relatively small, sitting among breaks in the cliffs. The most famous beaches can be found through a series of passages known as The Tunnels.

Ilfracombe Harbour viewed from Hillsborough

The town's harbour is enclosed by two piers, the larger of which is used as a car park. Ilfracombe was once a busy port until nearby Barnstaple and Bideford began to take over. The harbour was one of a few safe refuges for ships in the area.

On the summit of the 100-foot Lantern Hill, which sits above the harbour entrance, is a small chapel dedicated to St Nicholas, the patron saint of sailors. A light in the chapel has been guiding ships for more than 600 years. It was once occupied by a 13th-century hermit.

Opposite Lantern Hill on the other side of the harbour is another huge rocky mound known as Capstone Hill. A path entices walkers to reach its tip where upon they will be rewarded with breathtaking views. The climb is quite easy, though the hill is exposed and locals will tell you the north coast winds can be a little breezy to say the least!

Children will no doubt be tempted by the model village which sits at the foot of Torrs Walk – a popular hill climb of about one-and-a-half miles via zig-zag paths. From the top at about 500 feet you will get a fine view of the town and its Tunnel beaches directly below.

Torrs Walk is also where the coast path can be rejoined to take you across Lee Downs towards Lee Bay about two miles away.

The tiny village of **Lee** sits in Borough Valley – known to locals as Fuchsia Valley because of the colourful plants which grow here. In the village you will find the 17th-century thatched cottage which was supposed to have been occupied by the Old Maids of Lee in Fred Weatherley's famous song. Lee Bay is a sheltered cove and home to a rocky beach and large hotel.

The path from Lee Bay runs for about a mile-and-a-half along the cliff to **Bull Point** where a lighthouse guides ships in the Bristol Channel. It offers excellent views of the remote island of Lundy, and the Gower Peninsula some 30 miles away.

The path continues along the cliff over Rockham Bay for about a mile-and-a-half to **Morte Point** where you will sight Morte Bay and its famous Woolacombe Sands for the first time. The view extends all the way along the remaining North Devon coast on a clear day. Just off the Point is Morte Stone, also known as Death Stone, as it has been the downfall of many ships. According to legend any man who is master of his wife has power to move Morte Stone. Needless to say it has remained in the same position – and will do so for a very long time!

The village of **Mortehoe** is a mere half-mile inland and home to an ancient parish church where you will find the tomb of Sir William de Tracey. Contrary to popular belief this is not the de Tracey involved in the murder of Thomas a Becket, but a relative who lived nearly 200 years after the incident.

From Morte Point the path turns inland with the coast and then heads towards Grunta Beach about a mile away. This was once the scene of an unusual shipwreck consisting of a cargo of live pigs. Most of the animals were recaptured, though one of the pigs is believed to have lived freely on the beach for nearly a year, living on seaweed! Just around the corner is Barricane Beach which is famous for its sea shells.

The many rocks here soon make way for the three miles of golden sand which grace Woolacombe. The modern resort of **Woolacombe** is one of only three in North Devon which is home to a good sandy beach – the others can be found at Croyde and Saunton.

There is no doubting the beach is the main attraction and it is used as frequently by surfers as bathers. This stretch of coast, with its Atlantic rollers, provides some of the best surfing conditions in the country.

There are plenty of guest houses and hotels to cater for the visitor which will suit all tastes and pockets. Children will enjoy Once Upon a Time – a fairy tale theme park two miles inland.

The resort's church is dedicated to St Sabinus, who was an Irish missionary wrecked off the Woolacombe coast.

The main coast path runs along Woolacombe Down above the cliffs, though there are a number of paths leading down through dunes to the sea should you wish to stroll along the beach. At the end of Morte Bay the sands belong to Putsborough Beach. This secluded spot is another favourite haunt of windsurfers.

The path turns and heads towards Baggy Point where you will find more excellent views from the headland. It is a popular spot for 'twitchers' as it is home to a thriving population of sea birds. There are a number of caves here, including Baggy Hole which can be reached by boat during low tide.

From Baggy Point the path turns inland with the coast, dropping down to Croyde Bay less than a mile away. **Croyde** is home to another sandy beach, though it is nowhere near as large as the beaches at Woolacombe and Saunton which sit either side of it. Like many beaches in the area bathing during low tide is considered dangerous and visitors should take heed of the many warning signs. Otherwise, the beach at Croyde is a child's dream. Apart from its golden sand it is home to a number of fascinating rockpools.

The beautiful village itself is just as popular as the beach, but a lot smaller so its streets become very congested in the summer. Its charming thatched cottages and trickling stream, which runs along the road, create ideal picture-postcard shots.

The village is also home to the unusual Croyde Gem Rock and Shell Museum which displays gemstones from all over the world. It also contains giant clams from the South Pacific. Cutting and polishing demonstrations show visitors how the gems are turned into jewellery.

If the beaches at Croyde or Woolacombe become too packed there is always another three-mile stretch of beach at **Saunton Sands**. Motorists and walkers must travel the short distance along the B3231 road across Saunton Down to reach it. The path runs inland through Saunton and past its famous golf course which is home to a number of championship events. It then turns south and runs adjacent to the sea more than a mile away.

Braunton Burrows

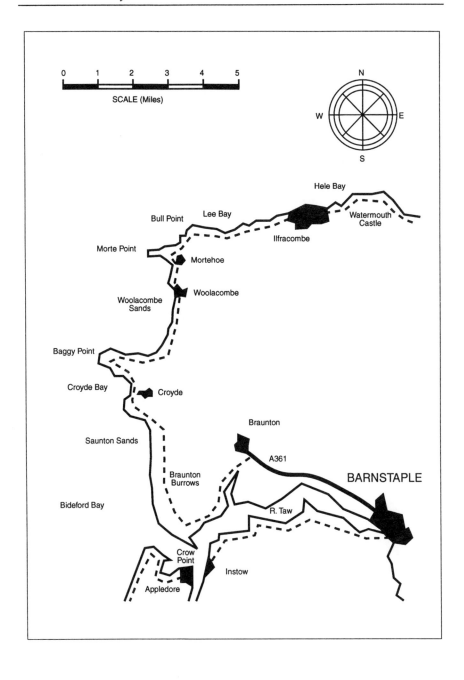

Saunton Sands is an impressive beach in itself, but it has an added attraction. It is backed by the extensive sand dunes belonging to the nature reserve known as **Braunton Burrows**.

The Burrows is home to a number of rare birds and wild flowers and is one of the largest sand dune areas in the country. The area is about a mile wide with some dunes reaching almost 100 feet in height. At times it is easy to imagine you are are walking in a desert wilderness. The area is also used as a Ministry of Defence range and so is closed to visitors when red flags are flying.

Saunton Sands and the Burrows run all the way to Crow Point where the Taw and Torridge rivers meet to form an estuary. Unfortunately, there is no longer a ferry operating across the estuary. The walker has no alternative but to follow the path inland to Braunton and join the road to Barnstaple which sits at the head of the Taw Estuary, six miles away.

Barnstaple is the largest town in North Devon and reputed to be the oldest borough in the country. From its early days as a busy working port it has developed into a modern market town with excellent shopping facilities. It is a popular base for visitors wishing to tour the north of the county and has plenty to offer itself.

From Barnstaple Bridge, which was built in 1350, you can get super views of the estuary. The bridge is better known as Long Bridge for it stretches 700 feet across the river. At its northern tip you will find The Square, with its attractive and well-kept lawns and flowers.

Next to the bus station on the estuary bank is the popular Queen Anne's Walk with its grand stone pillars and ornate carvings. It was built in 1609 and was once named Merchant's Walk as it was a favourite place to trade. Below the statue of Queen Anne sits the strange Tome Stone. The small stone table was used by merchants to strike a deal with shipowners. Once the money was placed on the table in full view of witnesses the deal was struck and it was too late for either party to change their mind.

One of the most distinctive buildings in Barnstaple is the

14th-century parish church of St Peter. Its lead-covered twisted spire is believed to have gained its abnormality through a bolt of lightning in 1810. The town is home to a number of historic buildings. The 17th-century Penrose Almshouses in Litchdon Street show their age through a bullet hole in one of the doors which is believed to have been made during the Civil War.

Queen Anne's Walk in Barnstaple was where merchants traded long ago

In Castle Street you might expect to find a castle, but you will be disappointed, for very little remains of the 8th-century fortress. The only visible evidence to its existence is the ruins of its 10-foot-thick walls once belonging to the keep which are hidden by trees on the central mound. The lines of the moat can also be traced.

If it is the town's history you seek then the place to go is St Anne's Chapel Museum. The building itself has many tales to tell as it is believed to have been the chapel of Irish missionary St Sabinus who was wrecked off the coast of Woolacombe. It was later used as the town's Grammar School, whose former pupils included Barnstaple-born poet John Gay – author of 'The Beggar's Opera'. The town's large Pannier market is also very popular, as is its cattle market which attracts farmers from all over North Devon.

The coast path on the south side of the estuary follows the old Barnstaple railway line along the bank of the River Taw. It runs all the way to **Instow** where there is a broad beach backed by more sand dunes. Bathing is popular here and waterskiing and sailing is also encouraged.

Pleasure boats at Appledore

The River Torridge provides the walker with another obstacle to cross, though fortunately a passenger ferry to Appledore operates in the summer. The alternative is to go inland and cross a bridge at Bideford five miles away.

The bustling town of **Bideford** sits on the bank of the Torridge Estuary. It was once one of the busiest ports in the country trading

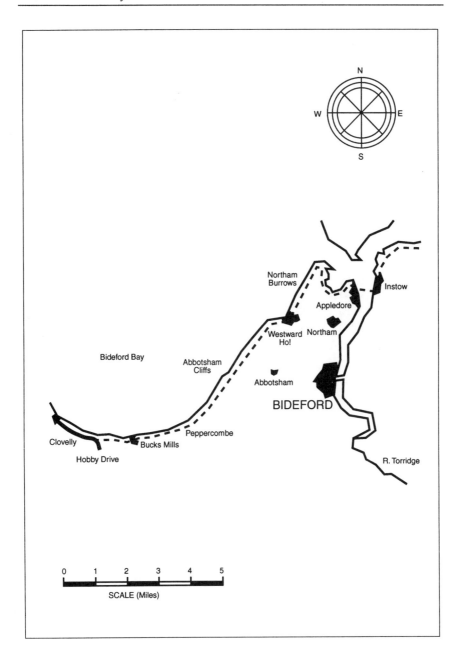

N
W   E
S

Northam
Burrows

Instow

Appledore

Westward   Northam
Ho!

Bideford Bay   Abbotsham
Cliffs

Abbotsham

BIDEFORD

Peppercombe

Clovelly   Bucks Mills

Hobby Drive

R. Torridge

0   1   2   3   4   5

SCALE (Miles)

with America, Europe and the West Indies. It was also the first port to import tobacco in large quantities.

Bideford's most famous landmark is its 677-foot bridge, complete with 24 arches, which replaced a ford in the 13th century. The original structure was made from wood, but covered in stone 200 years later. The long quay is lined with trees and makes a beautiful riverside walk. At the northern end of the quay you will find a statue of author Charles Kingsley, who wrote part of 'Westward Ho!' while living in the town.

Another fine walk is through the lush Victoria Park. Apart from putting and bowling facilities, it is home to a 16th-century cannon which is believed to have been captured from the Spanish Armada.

Apart from Kingsley there is at least one other famous person associated with the town. Sir Richard Grenville, explorer and captain of the Revenge, is remembered in the parish church of St Mary. He died in 1591 after being wounded fighting the Spanish off the coast of Azores. It is believed he lived in a house on the corner of Allhalland Street. Also in the church you will find a touching memorial to John Strange, who was mayor of Bideford on four occasions. It is believed to have been written by a shipwrecked sailor in gratitude of the kindness he received from Strange. The town had many reasons to thank Strange. On one occasion he took control of Bideford when the mayor at the time fled to escape the plague which arrived from Spain. Strange did all he could to get rid of the disease, but eventually became one of its victims.

Another 'strange' character – though he did not share the same name – was the potty, but wealthy Thomas Stucley, son of the chaplain of Oliver Cromwell. It is believed he drew plans of the Duke of Marlborough's sieges on the kitchen floor of his Bideford home using a pick-axe. After each conquest the floor had to be rebuilt!

A saner and more respected resident was 'postman poet' Edward Capern who resided in Mill Street and made his deliveries around town. The area of Bideford which sits across the river is known as East-the-Water. On the hill are the remains of Chudleigh Fort built by its namesake when Bideford, like Barnstaple, took the side of Parliament against the King during civil unrest. Excellent views of the town and surrounding area can be enjoyed from here.

The Pebble Ridge at Westward Ho! makes an ideal sun trap for holidaymakers

The coast path begins at the quay and heads back up the River Torridge. The three-and-a-half-mile stroll to Appledore provides one of the nicest walks in the area. The path sticks to the coast and slowly rises to give excellent views of the estuary. It also skirts **Northam** where you will find Bloody Corner – the spot where King Alfred supposedly fought a terrific battle with the Danes and killed King Hubba. A stone plaque commemorates the historic occasion.

The delightful fishing village of **Appledore** sits at the junction of the Taw and Torridge estuaries. It is a fascinating place with a maritime history going back more than a thousand years when Anglo-Saxons first fished from its shores. It was and still is a busy shipbuilding port, playing a big part in the defeat of the Spanish Armada in 1588 when it supplied ships and sailors. Queen Elizabeth is believed to have given it 'free port' status because of the vital role it played. The shipbuilding trade is still thriving today and Appledore is reputed to own the largest covered shipyard in Europe. Its shipyards also specialise in making full-size replicas of ships. These have included Viking longships, Roman galleys and Sir Francis Drake's *Golden Hind*. The area's maritime history can be retraced in the North Devon Maritime Museum where there is a special display on Appledore's links with Canada. Because of a shortage in wood, many local shipbuilders moved to Prince Edward Island in order to ply their trade.

There are a number of houses with good views of the estuary. Chanters Folly is a Medieval churchtower built by a merchant in 1800 to enable him to watch his ships come in over the horizon. With so many boats and so much water it is easy to neglect inland Appledore. But a walk around some delightful Georgian cottages and lanes, which are too narrow for cars, is well worth the trouble.

The Quay which is found to the west of the village is a superb viewing point. To the east you can look across to Braunton Burrows and up the estuary to Barnstaple, while a look the other way will give you a view across Bideford Bay to Hartland Point in the distance.

From Appledore the walker can head straight for Westward Ho! two miles away past the Royal North Devon Golf Club – one of the oldest in the country. Alternatively you can follow the coast path into Northam Burrows Country Park with its saltings and sand dunes. This walk will double the length of your journey, but there are nice views along the three-mile sands which join the beach at Westward Ho!

The most distinctive feature of **Westward Ho!** is the huge bank of shingle which shelters this stretch of coast. The grey-stone pebble ridge, known as the Popple, stretches for about two miles

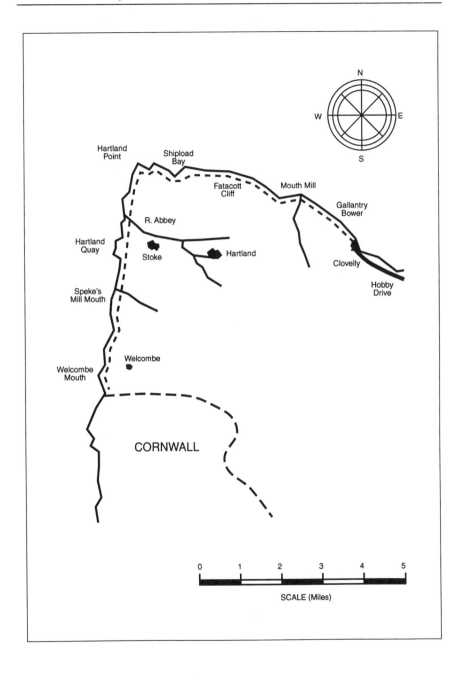

and is about 50 feet wide, reaching a height of 20 feet in places. Of course, the resort's other distinctive feature is its strange name. Westward Ho! is the only place in the country to be named after a novel and have an exclamation mark at the end of it! The novel in question was written by Charles Kingsley and follows the adventures of Elizabethan seafarers. The resort was founded in 1863 on the strength of the amazing success of Kingsley's book. Unfortunately things did not go to well in the early years. Among the early set-backs was the destruction of the resort's pier during a great storm.

Another building which soon disappeared was the United Services College which was closed and moved closer to London. It was at the college author Rudyard Kipling spent four years as a student from 1878. Reference to his time spent there can be found in his 'Stalky and Co' works. The building on the site today has been renamed Kipling Terrace in recognition of the great man's work.

Despite its poor start, Westward Ho! is now a thriving holiday centre. Bathers and surfers flock to its beach in the summer and there are a number of amusements for visitors.

The path from Westward Ho! climbs a cliff known as Kipling Tors, as it was here the young Rudyard spent many hours exploring caves. It hugs the coast for several miles along Abbotsham Cliffs which offer fine views of Bideford Bay. This stretch of coast all the way to Hartland Point, about 20 miles away, is home to a number of secluded grey-pebble beaches.

Once past Cockington Head, 350 feet above the sea, you will begin to enter Peppercombe and its beautiful wooded valley. There is a small shingle beach here which can be reached by a steep path. The main path passes a field which is the site of the ancient earthworks of Peppercombe Castle and through a mile of woodland before dropping to the small village of Bucks Mills.

Charming **Bucks Mills** sits in a wooded valley perched on the edge of the cliff. Its one main street is lined with attractive white-washed cottages and runs for half-a-mile from a car park to the sea. It is similar in appearance to Clovelly three miles along the coast, though it is not as popular, and unlike its neighbour, welcomes cars. The beach at the end of the street is a mixture of sand and shingle and also home to a number of rock pools.

The ruins of a 19th-century lime kiln overlook the beach. It was here limestone was brought from Wales; burned in the kilns and used by farmers to neutralise acidity in the soil.

The coastguard look-out once had the name Braund written on it. The Braunds, who once occupied the whole of the village, were believed to have originated from Spain and made their living fishing from these shores. Before organised lifeboat rescues they carried out their own service to struggling seamen.

The path from Bucks Mills climbs through one-and-a-half miles of woodland and fields before joining a scenic road known as Hobby Drive, which runs from Hobby Lodge on the edge of the A39 for three miles into Clovelly.

The beautiful private road was built as a hobby by Sir James Hamlyn-Williams, one-time owner of the estate. There is a toll fee for motorists which includes parking at the top of Clovelly.

The beautiful unspoilt village of **Clovelly** is one of the most delightful places in the country. It consists of just one cobbled street which plummets steeply down to the quay. White-washed thatched cottages, complete with colourful window boxes, cling to the steep hill as if they are about to topple over. The descent is so steep in places, the base of one cottage may be level with its neighbour's roof!

Cars are banned from entering the narrow street and even the villagers have to have their groceries delivered by sledge or donkey! Not surprisingly Clovelly's beauty has a drawback – tourists. It is only small but it is one of the most popular spots in Devon. In the summer the street, affectionately known as Up-a-Long and Down-a-Long, can become so crowded with visitors you almost have to queue to get to the beach! At the height of the holiday season it is believed about 7,000 people arrive in a day! The best time to visit is early morning or during the evening when most of the visitors have left.

Walking in Clovelly is no mean feat!

Fortunately, the usual tourist attractions, such as gift shops, are kept tucked away from the village at the visitors' centre and car park high above. There is however a Land Rover service which operates during the summer months to help disabled visitors enjoy the beauty of the village.

On many of the cottages you will no doubt notice the initials C.H. which stand for Christine Hamlyn. She owned the estate in the early part of this century, and following in her mother's footsteps, did all she could to protect the village's old-world charm by restoring old buildings to their former glory.

At the bottom of the street, if you reach that far (Remember you will have to walk back up!), you will find the village quay and a shingle beach with its popular Red Lion Hotel. The 14th-century quay was once very busy as it is the only refuge for ships between Westward Ho! and Bude. Today, the quay, which was built by George Cary, another former owner of the estate, is occupied by local fishermen and a few summer pleasure boats.

A strange memorial to George Cary's daughter, who died in 1655, can be found in Clovelly Church which is situated at the top of the village near Clovelly Court. It consists of a brass square depicting a skeleton holding a spade. Another brass in the church honours author Charles Kingsley who featured the village in 'Westward Ho!' and whose father was rector of Clovelly in the 1830s. Another famous novelist inspired by Clovelly's charms was Charles Dickens who referred to it as 'Steepways' in his Christmas story 'A Message from the Sea'.

The surrounding woodland, much of which is owned by the National Trust, includes a fine viewing area known as Mount Pleasant. It was given to the people by Mrs Hamlyn as a memorial to the villagers who lost their lives during the First World War.

The coast path, which can be picked up at Mount Pleasant, runs through the grounds of Clovelly Court. It enters woodland and passes the ornate Angels' Wings about a mile away. The beautifully-carved wooden garden seat and shelter is an ideal place to rest your weary feet.

Less than half-a-mile away is the dramatic 400-foot headland known as Gallantry Bower. **Gallantry Bower** is believed to have got its name from the many desperate lovers who held hands and jumped from the cliff when they were forbidden to marry. Others, perhaps the less romantic, say it was simply the site of the old village gallows.

Just past Gallantry Bower are some steps which lead to a small tunnel in the cliff. It runs to an artificially-cut viewing point where you will find Miss Woodall's seat. Miss Woodall created the 'balcony' so she could enjoy the splendid view out to sea. From here the path climbs another cliff overlooking Mouth Mill, less than a mile away.

Mouth Mill and its tiny cove is backed by glorious sloping hills. A tiny stream runs inland from the sea through the woods providing a charming walk for those wishing to follow it. The rocks at Mouth Mill are impressive. Among them is the 80-foot Blackchurch Rock with its two natural arches.

The path from Mouth Mill leads to the earthworks at Windbury Head and onto Exmansworthy Cliff which towers more than 500 feet above the sea. There are excellent views of Blackchurch Rock and Gallantry Bower from this impressive vantage point. The highest point can be found a short distance along at Fatacott Cliff. About a mile from here is the sheltered Shipload Bay which gives the walker a rare opportunity to venture down onto the shore via a long steep path. There you will find a sand and shingle beach and some twisted rocks to the right at Eldern Point. The path then passes a radar station at West Titchberry Cliff before running to the gates of Hartland Point Lighthouse a mile away.

The remote and dramatic **Hartland Point** is one of the most desolate places in the county. It stands 325 feet above the raging Atlantic Ocean which pounds relentlessly at the ragged rocks below. The Romans called it the 'Promontory of Hercules' – and it is easy to see why! The sight of the crashing waves on a stormy day is an awe-inspiring experience and something to savour

At the highest point of the headland is a coastguard station.

From here a path drops down to Hartland Point Lighthouse standing on a perch about 100 feet above the sea.

Most people come to Hartland Point to take in the tremendous views. On a good day the coast of Wales is clearly visible some 40 miles away. A little closer is Lundy which is about 12 miles from here. An occasional helicopter flies visitors across to the island during the summer.

The coast path turns south along the cliff and after a mile crosses Abbey River, which leads to Hartland Abbey two miles inland. You can judge the two-mile walk to Hartland Quay by the ruined Warren Tower which is visible from miles around. It was believed to be used as a look-out by pirates.

Hartland Quay is just as impressive as the Point, with yet more contorted rocks emerging from the sea. The harbour was first built by the monks of Hartland Abbey in the 15th century to provide a refuge for ships. In the next century it was strengthened under the direction of three of the country's greatest seafarers – Sir Walter Raleigh, Sir Francis Drake and Sir John Hawkins. Unfortunately it was not strong enough to withstand some tremendous gales at the end of the 19th century and most of it was swept away. Today, the quay is a little more hospitable with a hotel, swimming pool and small museum gracing its shores.

About a mile inland is the tiny village of **Stoke** which is home to Hartland's enormous parish church – the highest in Devon. The impressive 130-foot St Nectan's Church was built as a landmark for ships in the 14th century which explains why it can be seen from miles around. It is named after a Welsh missionary who was murdered here during the 6th century.

Inside you will find a lavish 15th-century screen, which at more than 45 feet is believed to be the largest in Devon. You will also find a memorial to publisher Sir Allen Lane who founded the hugely-successful Penguin Books.

The parish of Hartland is the second largest in Devon and covers about 14 miles. The actual market town of Hartland is about three miles inland from Hartland Quay.

Hartland Point Lighthouse

From Hartland Quay the path continues south, hugging the coast closely. This stretch of coastline is known as the Iron Coast. It is home to a number of tiny inlets and beautiful streams which plunge over the cliff as waterfalls. One of the most spectacular can be found at **Speke's Mill Mouth** about a mile south of the quay. There is a shingle and rocky beach here which is reached by a steep path.

The main path continues south over a stretch of coast believed to be the least visited on the entire coast path. The reason is because there are no built-up villages or towns anywhere near. The path runs for three miles before reaching Welcombe Mouth.

At **Welcombe Mouth** there is a sand and pebble beach with a nature reserve behind it. This was the hunting ground of 'Cruel' Coppinger – a notorious 18th-century smuggler and wrecker from Denmark.

The beach at Welcombe Mouth can also be reached by a narrow road just off the A39. That road will also take you into the tiny village of Welcombe itself. The hamlet of cottages is appropriately named as it is usually the first place visitors reach when crossing into Devon from Cornwall. The Devon-Cornwall border is half-a-mile away, marked by the beautiful combe of Marshland Mouth.

The long-distance walker should be aware there is no public transport here and so they may have to walk a further eight miles into Bude on the North Cornwall coast to complete their trek.

The Seaside

The rise of Devon's resorts

Very little can beat a British holiday at the seaside. Every year thousands of people flock to our beaches armed with their bucket and spade and for at least two weeks, the smell of fish and chips and the tuneful beeps from the amusement arcades become a way of life to them.

It is therefore surprising the seaside holiday is a relatively new idea. Before the 17th century the idea of visiting the sea for pleasure was unimaginable. People living within just a few miles of a sandy shore may not have even visited it during their entire life! The sea was a dangerous place and those who ventured near it did so out of necessity, usually to catch fish to earn a living.

Of course, most people could not afford, or even had the time, for a holiday. The average man worked six days a week and it would be nothing short of scandalous for him to spend his Sunday anywhere but in church. The early visitors to the sea only came to improve their health. Inland spa resorts, such as the one at Bath, were popular during the 17th century when people took the spring water believing it to be a cure for many ailments. Medical experts soon began to believe the sea also contained the necessary salts to cure disease and encouraged the ill to descend to the coast. Certainly, the last thing on these early visitors' minds was to go and enjoy themselves. Bathers often had to be physically forced to enter the icy water!

The early health resorts, as they became known, began to advertise the supposed quality of their sea water and made extravagant claims it could cure almost any ailment. It is perhaps ironic in this day and age, when the Government is doing its best to allay polluted water fears, that the early Victorians were told sea water was a healthy medicine – and were encouraged to drink it in large doses! At Teignmouth, one of the earliest health resorts, it was claimed lepers could be cleansed and cripples could be made to walk again. At the end of the 18th century an Exeter newspaper reported the story of an elderly crippled clergyman who gained the use of both his hands and legs after drinking the Teignmouth sea water.

The first coastal health resorts in Britain were believed to have been at Brighton, Margate and Scarborough where bathing was reported during the 1730s. Devon was not far behind with the village of Exmouth being recognised as a health resort by the mid-18th century. It became popular because of its close proximity to the city of Exeter. At the time Exeter had a thriving woollen trade and people were beginning to be able to afford to take holidays and travel to the coast – their nearest place being Exmouth. In less than a decade, the visitors began to spread their wings and travel further down the coast to Teignmouth and Dawlish, and eastwards to Sidmouth.

Teignmouth Pier once acted as a segregation point for male and female bathers

The north coast of Devon developed much more slowly as the area was sparsely populated and mostly made up of farmers who could not afford to travel. Poor inaccessible roads also limited travelling. During the mid-18th century it took coaches from Exeter to Barnstaple at least half-a-day to cover the 40-mile distance!

Poor roads throughout the country meant the early seaside visitors came from within the county. The journey from London to Exeter could take up to four days by coach and so the capital's gentry chose to visit their nearby resorts in Kent and Sussex. Travelling abroad to France was often easier and those who could afford it preferred to do so. It was the French Revolution at the end of the 18th century and war with France at the beginning of the next which put paid to this and gave English health resorts a major boost.

Ordinary working class people still could not afford a holiday, even though smaller, less fashionable resorts did begin to appear to offer an alternative to the pricey established resorts. The likes of Seaton and Budleigh Salterton never pretended to offer the same facilities which were being provided by their bigger rivals and so proved to be an attractive alternative to the average man. Even so, these too began to grow and received more distinguished visitors as they did so.

The North Devon coast also offered a cheap solution and by the end of the 18th century bathing had been reported at Ilfracombe, Instow and Appledore. These places were all close to the towns of Barnstaple and Bideford and very few early visitors came from anywhere else. Those who did would often arrive by a steamer from Bristol as this was easier than travelling by road. Improved roads and the arrival of the railway finally put the north coast on the map in the mid-19th century.

People soon began to visit the seaside for enjoyment rather than to improve their health. The twin resorts of Lynton and Lynmouth on the edge of Exmoor became two of the first places to be visited simply for their beauty. The Romantic poets, such as Coleridge, Wordsworth, Southey and Shelley, were all drawn to it for inspiration and their work encouraged others. R.D. Black-more's hugely-successful 'Lorna Doone' also helped attract visitors wishing to explore the many places featured in his classic book, most of whom used Lynton and Lynmouth as a base.

Slowly, amusements such as golf and bowls were provided to entertain visitors. Promenades became popular in the late 18th century and enabled the rich to parade the latest fashions. Strangely, they were not always built by the sea. At Exmouth the original promenade was built on Beacon Hill. Most promenades were constructed to allow invalids to be pushed in their wheelchairs so they could take in the fresh air even if they were too ill to enter the water.

The early bathers were often segregated. At Dawlish, the ladies bathed on the main beach, while the men bathed around the corner of the headland at Coryton Cove. Resorts lucky enough to have a pier often used this to divide the two sexes as in the case at Teignmouth. It was not until the end of the 19th century mixed bathing became accepted – Seaton and Paignton being the first resorts in Devon to take the plunge. The rest soon followed suit.

Bathing machines also helped preserve the bather's dignity. These were sheds built on wheels which could be pushed out into the sea so the bather could change into their costume and step straight into the water without being viewed.

Piers were originally built to cope with the growing demand of pleasure boats. Today, there are very few still standing and most of these have become an extension of the promenade with yet more amusement arcades! Four promenade piers were built in Devon – the first being the 600-foot Grand Pier at Teignmouth in 1867. Another followed at Westward Ho! in 1873, but this was destroyed by a storm. The longest pier in the county was built in 1879 at Paignton and stretched nearly 800 feet. The last to be built was a stone pier at Torquay in 1895.

Of course, Devon's most popular resort today is undoubtedly Torquay. Though it was a late starter, its popularity soon rocketed because of its exceptional mild climate. In the mid-19th century its population tripled in 20 years! Its south-facing, sheltered position ensured it had an excellent climate all year round and it soon became the country's principal winter health resort.

Ironically, Torquay's mild temperatures almost proved to be its downfall at one stage as many people complained it was too hot! Victorians favoured pale skin and so the high temperatures frightened and deterred people from visiting during the summer. The town had to do its best to encourage tourists by playing down its mild climate. Guidebooks actually tried to produce statistics to convince people the summer temperatures in Torquay were lower than in many other resorts!

In 1871, the Government passed the Bank Holiday Act which gave people even more time to enjoy a trip to the seaside. The highest number of visitors to a Devon seaside resort during the 19th century was at Exmouth on August Bank Holiday 1897 when 6,000 people arrived. This figure was still small compared to other resorts around the country – the increasingly popular Blackpool claimed to have nearly 40,000 people at the same time!

One resort which failed to attract anything like this number was the unique Westward Ho! on the north coast of Devon. It was unique because, while most resorts evolved around existing settlements, Westward Ho! was created on previously uninhabited land. It was named after Charles Kingsley's epic novel, though he was said to be stunned when he learned a resort was going to be built on Northam Burrows because of the success of his book. He was also horrified to discover his favourite stretch of coast was to make way for a holiday camp! Nevertheless, the foundation stone was laid in 1863 and the resort was labelled the future Torquay of the north coast. Bathing machines were introduced and hot and cold water baths were opened. Despite a top publicity campaign the resort never took off and was plagued by a number of catastrophes. These included a water pollution scare and the destruction of the newly-built pier and many houses during a great storm. Westward Ho! only became popular after the Second World War.

Looking at Westward Ho! and other thriving resorts today it is difficult to imagine the seaside was once looked at with awe. Of course, today's resorts are scarcely recognisable as the ones which first enticed visitors to their shores. Fancy lights and hi-tech amusements have all but transformed them and one can only wonder what the next 100 years has in store!

Shipwrecks

The harsher side of Devon's coast

Look out to sea on a calm summer's day and you will find it difficult to believe hundreds off ill-fated boats and ships are rotting away on the seabed. But Devon, with so many miles of coastline, has not surprisingly had more than its fair share of unlucky vessels succumbing to its hazardous rocks.

One of the most notorious stretches of the South Devon coast is between Bolt Tail and Bolt Head where hundreds of vessels have been destroyed. The most costliest was the warship *HMS Ramillies* which went down just east of Bolt Tail in 1760 taking more than 700 men with it. Helpless onlookers from the cliff watched horrified as enormous waves swept over the ship and tossed hundreds into the water. Only 26 survived the tragedy, which at the time was described as the greatest Royal Navy disaster ever.

The crew and passengers of the *Jebba*, which was wrecked here during thick fog in 1907, were a little more fortunate and all 155 were brought to safety. They had two locals to thank, for they climbed down a 200-foot cliff in darkness to rig up a bosun's chair and lift the crew to safety.

The most famous wreck in this area occurred in 1936 when the Finnish barque *Herzogin Cecilie* hit Ham Stone and grounded near Soar Mill Cove. The 3,000-tonne vessel was known as the Duchess because of her figurehead of the Duchess Cecilie, daughter of the Duke of Oldenburg. She gained fame after smashing the speed record for a sailing ship when she covered 2,120 nautical miles in seven days while sailing from Australia to Chile.

The battle to save the Duchess after she struck Ham Stone became national news. Holes were temporarily patched and she was towed into Starehole Bay at the mouth of Salcombe Harbour. But disaster struck again just seven weeks later when a ferocious storm broke and gave the ill-fated ship another battering. By the following morning she had vanished and sightseers could only make out a dark shape under the water.

The reason why the Duchess was so far off-course in the first place – about ten miles north of her intended line – was because of an inaccurate ship's compass. Many captains gave this excuse when they wrecked their ships on this stretch of coast, leading to the theory the ships' compasses may have been affected by iron which was regularly mined on the cliffs between Bigbury and Prawle Point.

The quiet resort of Hope Cove, sitting below Bolt Tail, was the scene of the only known wreck of an Armada ship on the English coast. The 580-tonne *San Pedro* was a supply and transport ship which became separated from the Armada during fierce fighting in 1588. Those on board, which included about 50 wounded soldiers, did not have enough strength to sail her and so she drifted aimlessly in the wind. It is believed she circumnavigated Britain before drifting back to Plymouth and down to Hope Cove where she crashed on Shippen Rock. Most of the crew, with their last ounce of strength, clambered ashore, but received little help from the locals as they were too busy plundering the ship's loot. Those who did make it to shore were taken as prisoners.

The sight of a ship floundering within metres of the shore must have been a harrowing experience. In 1691, 600 men were killed when *HMS Coronation* capsized within sight of Plymouth Sound. The ship was just one of a number in a fleet which decided to risk getting back to shore when a fierce storm broke instead of dropping anchor until it had subsided.

The north coast of Devon has also had a reputation for being one of the most dangerous areas in the country and has claimed its fair share of victims. One of the more tragic incidents occurred in 1799 when all 105 crew members aboard *HMS Weazle* died during a great storm in Bideford Bay. The ship was engaged in the battle against the smuggling trade and had been docked at

Appledore for several weeks. It was particularly tragic because the crew and locals had thrown a farewell party the night before. During their stay the crew had made friends with the locals and it was with great regret they left the following morning bound for Falmouth. A large crowd gathered on the shore to wave them off, for what was quite literally to be the final time. As the ship headed towards Hartland Point it was caught in a ferocious storm. It fired its guns as a distress signal on the hour throughout the early part of the night, until 1am when everything fell silent. The ship had crashed into rocks at Baggy Point. The wreck was discovered on a beach in Croyde Bay the following morning.

The people of Appledore were devastated and held a special funeral service in Bideford. A memorial to the dead can still be seen at Northam Church. The first stanza of a poem written shortly after the tragedy summed up the feelings of the people:

'Lament for the Weazle,
The joy of our bay;
Whose trim was so gallant;
Whose crew were so gay;
Hearts that never knew fear,
Yet confessed beauty's eye,-
Then rain beauty's tear,
For the day-dream gone by!'

Among the bodies washed ashore was that of a woman. As no ladies were allowed on board, she was believed to have been an unlucky stowaway. At least one crew member was lucky, however. This man had missed the sailing – some say because he was suffering the effects of the party the night before!

The weather has destroyed thousands of vessels over the years – and even the normally mild English Riviera has not escaped the full force of it. One night in 1866, a mini hurricane swept the coast around Torbay destroying about 50 ships and claiming the lives of about 100 men. The damage was so bad it was claimed people could walk all along the wreckage on the south west side of the bay the following morning.

The cost of wrecks is always counted on human lives and quite rightly, but the financial cost has also been huge in some cases. In 1906, the massive battleship *HMS Montagu* came to grief on rocks on the southern tip of Lundy during thick fog. The Royal Navy's pride and joy cost £1 million to build. Fortunately, all 750 crew were saved, but the ship was lost for ever.

The Royal National Lifeboat Institution was formed in 1824 by Sir William Hillary, a member of the crew of the Douglas, Isle of Man, lifeboat. The national service ended localised efforts to save those in trouble at sea, which had gone on for centuries.

One amazing rescue which involved a whole community occurred on the North Devon coast during a stormy winter's night in 1899. The 2,000-tonne *Forest Hall* was drifting towards the dangerous Exmoor coast at Countisbury when the crew sent a red flare into the misty night sky. The distress signal was spotted at Lynmouth, but the storm was so bad it was impossible to launch the lifeboat. There was no alternative but to carry the ten-tonne lifeboat Louisa across land on a 15-mile journey and launch it closer to where the signal had been spotted. Twenty horses and about 100 villagers, including women and children, began the long trek in atrocious conditions, believing the lives of the seamen depended on them. Their main obstacle was the awesome Countisbury Hill. Its summit at 1,300 feet had to be reached by negotiating a one-in-three gradient. Inch by inch they struggled to reach the top, fearful for their own lives should the mighty boat on its carriage begin to roll back down. They arrived at Porlock eight hours after setting off and were able to launch the boat and reach the crew of the Forest Hall. Ironically, many now believe it was a wasted journey as the Forest Hall was intact when they arrived and had already been reached by two tugs.

There are countless stories in which brave lifeboatmen have risked their lives – and often lost them – trying to save others. Perhaps the most tragic waste of life occurred at Salcombe in 1916. The lifeboat was launched to come to the rescue of the *Western Lass*, a Plymouth schooner floundering in Lannacombe Bay. Unknown to lifeboatmen at the time, the crew of the schooner had already been rescued by coastguards at Prawle. After battling against enormous waves, the Salcombe Lifeboat reached the wreck, and seeing nobody on board, began to make their way back. But the gigantic waves were too powerful and their boat was turned onto its side. Just two of the 15 lifeboatmen survived the tragedy. The lost 13 are remembered on a memorial at the resort's Cliff House Gardens.

Of course, it is not just the weather which has destroyed ships and many have been purposely wrecked – either by 19th-century wreckers or enemy warships during times of war. During the First World War many warships were sunk off the south coast at Start Bay – victims of undetected German submarines in the Channel. In 1925, the British submarine M-1 was literally lost after a training exercise in Start Bay. Despite a major search, the exact location was never traced and the 69 crew were officially pronounced dead. The Germans were also known to have lost at least three U-boats in the Start Point area.

Some ships have laid undiscovered for many years – and in some cases for centuries! Hope Cove, as mentioned earlier, was believed to be the only site of an Armada shipwreck on the English coast, though this may not be the case. In the summer of 1975, schoolboy Simon Burton made an amazing discovery while scuba diving off the coast of Teignmouth. Lying half-buried on the seabed was a one-and-a-half-tonne bronze cannon believed to be hundreds of years old. In the following years further treasures were discovered, including a gold seal now stored at Teignmouth Museum. It led experts to conclude young Burton's bounty may have come from the wreck of a small, but heavily armed, private enterprise vessel sailing with the Spanish Armada.

The ship still lies in its watery grave hundreds of years after it sunk. No doubt it shares the seabed with many more forgotten vessels – all victims of the harsher side of Devon's beautiful coast.

Lighthouses

The guiding lights of Devon

Lighthouses have sat on lonely cliff-tops, flashing their warning signals for at least three centuries. Hundreds of sailors have had these unique solitary beacons to thank for their lives.

Man has of course been guiding ships long before the first lighthouse was lit on British shores. Early warning signals appeared in the form of open fires and this method of signalling continued for centuries. The world's first recorded lighthouse was the Pharos of Alexandria built in the 3rd century BC. It was more than 300 feet high and its light came from an open fire at the tip of its tower.

One of the earliest known warning lights in Devon appeared at Ilfracombe in the 13th century. The 100-foot Lantern Hill, which rises above the harbour, is home to the chapel of St Nicholas which has been burning a warning light for sailors for more than 600 years. During Medieval times churches often doubled up as lighthouses and were commonly occupied by hermits. Unfortunately, most of these lights were extinguished at the dissolution of the monasteries. The light at Ilfracombe is one of a few exceptions.

During the 13th century the Archbishop of Canterbury formed a guild of seamen, whose jobs included building and lighting beacons to guide mariners. The guild later became known as Trinity House. However, it was not until the mid-16th century that the first lighthouses were built in Britain – at Tynemouth and North Shields.

Lighting the shore was a slow process and the country still only had 11 lighthouses when the 18th century began. All of these were on the south and east coast and there there were none in Devon and Cornwall despite the reputation its dangerous coastline was beginning to earn. Even so, work had begun on the world's first ever rock station lighthouse at Eddystone Rock 14 miles from Plymouth, which had been the scene of a number of wrecks. It was completed in 1698, but as we will see later, was plagued with problems.

London-based Trinity House was eventually given the exclusive right to erect lighthouses and many more began to appear during the late 18th century. The boom period was between 1870 and 1900 when about 50 lighthouses were erected. By the beginning of the 20th century there was a lighthouse at almost every 20 miles on the coast of England.

The early lighthouses consisted of a coal fire in a metal basket at the top of an open tower. The lighthouse keeper would often have difficulty controlling the fire during strong winds. The light would burn tons of coal and often melt the metal fence around it, such was the intensity at which it burned. Candles were soon introduced, but these lacked power. At Eddystone at least 24 candles had to be lit simultaneously and the keeper was required to snuff the wicks every 30 minutes. The major breakthrough came in 1782 when Aime Argand invented the first oil burner suitable for lighting purposes.

Of course, electricity is used to light the lamp these days, though the intensity of a lighthouse beam is still measured in candlepower. The most powerful Trinity House light can be found at St Catherine's Point on the Isle of White. Its light has an intensity of five-and-a-quarter million candela and a range of 26 miles. Most of Devon's lighthouses have a range of about 20 miles.

During the 19th century small towers began to crop up at the entrance of harbours to aid fishing boats. An early example can be seen at Lynmouth in the form of the Rhenish Tower which still acts as a navigational aid to fishermen.

One of Devon's earliest lighthouses was lit at Braunton in 1820. The light could be adjusted to indicate the safest channel between Bideford bar which was ever-changing due to shifting sands. Like many around the country it was demolished in 1957. Today the bar is lit by lights at Instow and a light in a small tower at Crow Point. Devon still has a number of lighthouses perched on its hazardous coastline. The principal lights are featured in the next few pages:

Eddystone Rock Lighthouse

Eddystone Rock lies about 14 miles south west of Plymouth. It caused the death of many a ship during Stuart times, prompting the authorities to build a warning tower which was to become the world's first rock station lighthouse. Its exposed position was under-estimated and it took several attempts to build a lighthouse strong enough to resist the constant battering from the sea.

The original Eddystone Lighthouse was first lit in 1698 and consisted of an 80-foot wood and stone tower. It did not last long, for its designer Henry Winstanley considered it to be too small and had it replaced within a year by a new elaborate 100-foot building with a 25-foot diameter. At £8,000 people considered it to be an engineering masterpiece – until a great storm in 1703 completely destroyed it!

London silk merchant John Rudyard was next to try his luck, building an even stronger lighthouse six years later. The wooden tower was held to the rock by 36 huge bolts which were sealed with red-hot pewter. It stood for almost 50 years until it was also destroyed – this time by fire. One of the three keepers on duty during the fateful night died nearly two weeks later after complaining he had swallowed some of the molten lead. Few believed him, but during the post mortem almost half-a-pound of lead was found in his stomach!

It was then the turn of engineer John Smeaton. He decided the lighthouse should be built entirely with stone. On its completion almost 1,000 tonnes of granite, shipped from Exmoor and Dartmoor, had been used to build it. Not surprisingly it stood for more than a century, until 1870 when the chief engineer for Trinity House James Douglass was asked to design a new lighthouse. Smeaton's tower was moved stone by stone to Plymouth Hoe where it remains today as a memorial to its builder. Visitors can climb to the top and on a clear day can see the present Eddystone Lighthouse 14 miles away.

Smeaton's Tower on Plymouth Hoe once stood exposed on Eddystone Rock

Douglass's new tower was built on a larger rock at Eddystone. The foundation stone was laid by the Duke of Edinburgh in 1878 and he returned to lay the final stone three years later.

Start Point Lighthouse

The lighthouse at Start Point sits on one of the most exposed peninsulas on the English coast. It was designed by Trinity House engineer James Walker and established in 1836. The original light was found to be inadequate in fog and so a bell was fitted in the 1860s. It was replaced by a siren just 15 years later.

The lighthouse machinery was operated by a weight which fell in a tube running down a sheer cliff. Start Point Lighthouse was fully automated in 1993 and is now controlled from St Catherine's Lighthouse on the Isle of White.

Berry Head Lighthouse

The highest, smallest and deepest lighthouse in the country was established in 1906. The tower barely reaches 15 feet, but there is no need for it to reach any higher as it is perched 200 feet above the sea on Berry Head cliff.

The light is now turned by a small motor, but like Start Point was originally turned with the help of a weight which was dropped about 150 feet down a deep shaft. The lighthouse itself is not spectacular, but the view from the cliff-top is superb and stretches as far as Portland Bill on the Dorset coast.

Foreland Point Lighthouse

Established in 1900, Foreland Point Lighthouse is perched on the side of the cliff. Like Berry Head, the tower is relatively small, but it stands high above the sea. It can be reached by a well-trodden path about half-a-mile from the main coast path. Its light has an intensity of one million candela – the most powerful of any Devon lighthouse.

Bull Point Lighthouse

The original Bull Point Lighthouse was established on the headland near the village of Mortehoe in 1879. It stood without any
problems for nearly 100 years. Then, in September 1972, the
lighthouse keeper reported cracks in the tower and claimed the
ground in the engine room appeared to be moving. Within a week
part of the cliff collapsed into the sea taking the fog signal house
with it.

A former Trinity House tower, which once stood at Braunton
Sands, was used as a temporary light until work was completed
on a new lighthouse in 1974 at a cost of £71,000. The new
lighthouse is fully automatic, but still managed by a keeper living
in the cottage beside it.

Hartland Point Lighthouse

The remote Hartland Point Lighthouse sits perched on a stone
ledge at the bottom of the cliff. Because of its dramatic position,
it has become one of the most popular tourist attractions in
Devon. It was a different story when it was built in 1874, however.
A road had to be especially cut into the cliff to reach the point
where the lighthouse was to be built and all the original surveying
was done off-shore in a boat!

The exposed Hartland Point takes the full brunt of the Atlantic
storms and suffered such a battering over the years that rock had
to be taken from the cliff beside the lighthouse and put on the
beach below to form a barrier against the sea. Unfortunately, the
natural barrier was not strong enough and the boulders were
washed away. A sea wall – 130 feet long and 19 feet high – had
to be built in 1925 to do the job.

Hartland Point Lighthouse was managed by four keepers until
automation in 1984. It is now monitored by keepers at Nash Point
Lighthouse in Mid-Glamorgan.

Bull Point Lighthouse

Smuggling

A thriving trade on the coast of Devon

Smuggling has always had a certain amount of romance attached to it. Daring men landing booty on remote shores during stormy, moonless nights conjures up an exciting and glamorous image. Certainly, those who took part in the smuggling trade often became mini-celebrities – and the likes of Beer smuggler John Rattenbury became living legends.

It was when duty was put on goods during Medieval times that first prompted men to risk their lives in the dead of night, though it was not until the 18th century smuggling peaked to extraordinary heights. Devon, with its two coastlines containing numerous inlets, estuaries and secluded coves, was no exception – and almost everybody was at it!

Boats now occupy the shore at Beer where smugglers once landed their booty

Many smugglers believed they were actually offering a service to the community. Because they did not pay duty, they could sell the goods at a cheaper price. Most villagers jumped at the chance to obtain cheap tea, brandy and tobacco – luxuries they would otherwise be unable to afford. To be successful, smugglers had to have contacts and these often came from the most unlikely sources; from squires to members of the clergy. As Rudyard Kipling wrote: 'brandy for the parson, baccy for the clerk!' Churches were excellent places to store contraband. The church at Thurlestone was just one ecclesiastical building which put its high roof to good use, regularly storing kegs of brandy.

The most famous men of the cloth who took part in the smuggling trade were two former vicars of East Budleigh. The Rev Matthew Mundy who served from 1741-1794, and the Rev Ambrose Stapleton, who followed until 1852, used the vicarage for more than writing sermons and would secretly meet their fellow colleagues there to plan their many excursions along the coast!

Smugglers would ship all sorts of cargo ashore to sell for a profit, and most people were happy to let it happen – apart from the Government, of course! In a bid to thwart the 'traders of the night,' as the smugglers were affectionately known, customs officers began to patrol the coast in cutters, though the smugglers were often too clever for them and so it was to little success.

Many men would be involved in each operation and so it would only take a matter of minutes once the ship had landed. The incoming ship would receive signals from a spotsman stationed on top of the cliffs. When it was safe to come ashore he would flash a spout lantern which could only be seen from out at sea. There was usually nobody about, for the smugglers worked in the darkest and stormiest nights, which not even the Revenue cutters would dare venture out into.

The most famous Devon smuggler was the dashing John Rattenbury, born in the village of Beer in 1778. He became a local legend for his many scrapes with the authorities during a 40-year reign. Customs officers were always hot on his trail, but rarely caught the elusive Rattenbury. On the few occasions they did, he would usually find a way to escape from their clutches. Despite his apparent success, Rattenbury died a poor man which proved the profits of the trade were not as good as one would have supposed. Frequent bumbled operations meant valuable cargo was often lost at sea to great expense. Rattenbury smuggled all sorts of items; from liquor to tobacco – and even French prisoners on one occasion, though this was unsuccessful.

His amazing exploits were recorded in his own diary, which was published as a book in 1837 entitled 'Memoirs of a Smuggler'. In it was his most famous escape from the clutches of the authorities which occurred in a pub in his home village. Rattenbury was drinking with friends when a group of soldiers in the inn discovered his identity. Once they had armed themselves, the soldiers attempted to apprehend him. The startled smuggler fled to the cellar and waited with his knife in hand ready to confront his aggressors. Despite being outnumbered by a dozen men, armed with swords and muskets, Rattenbury insisted he would fight to the death and kill anyone who came near him. The sergeant ordered his men to seize Rattenbury, but only received a terrified reply that he had proposed the attack and should therefore do so himself! Not surprisingly the equally apprehensive sergeant stayed put and a four-hour stalemate developed until Rattenbury took his chance to flee past them when they were pre-occupied with some other business.

Whether the story is totally accurate, it is difficult to say, but it certainly highlights the enormous and respected reputation Rattenbury earned himself. His memoirs were published while smuggling was still thriving and so it is not surprising he never revealed many tips, or the names of his former associates who were still plying their trade!

Evidence of Devon's thriving smuggling era can be found all along the coastline. Apart from smugglers' lanes and tunnels – such as the one leading to Ness Beach at Shaldon – many coves and rocks are named after the period. Samson's Bay, about a mile east of Ilfracombe, is named after a smuggler who stored contraband in a cave, while to the west is Brandy Cove – named after the goods that were landed. Ralph's Hole, a cove near Bolt Tail on the south coast, is also named after a famous smuggler known simply by his Christian name. It was in a cave near here Ralph held off advancing customs officers with a pitchfork!

The dangers faced by the excisemen is highlighted at Smuggler's Leap – a precipice on the cliffs close to the village of Martinhoe. It was here a dramatic cliff-top chase on horses ended in tragedy. The customs officer drew alongside the smuggler's horse and reached out to grab hold of the assailant. As he did so, the smuggler turned his frightened horse towards the cliff-edge and plunged over the top, taking the officer with him. Their dead bodies were discovered on the rocks below, still in a position of fixed combat.

In the parish church of Branscombe you will see another permanent reminder of the dangers of those who sought to thwart the smugglers. The epitaph reads:

'Here lieth the body of Mr John Hurley, Custom House Officer of this Parish. As he was endeavouring to extinguish some fire made between Beer and Seaton as a signal to a smuggling boat then off at sea he fell by some means or other from the top of the cliff to the bottom by which he was unfortunately killed. This unhappy accident happened the 5th day of August in the year of our Lord 1755. Aetatis suae 45. He was an active and diligent officer and very inoffensive in his life and conversation.'

In 1817, nine seamen were killed while on the look-out for smugglers off the coast of Sidmouth. Their boat, the Queen Charlotte, was caught in a storm and all the men drowned. Midshipman William Paulson and his eight crew members are remembered on an epitaph on the wall of Seaton Parish Church.

Another famous smuggler who gave the excisemen a torrid time – though with less tragic consequences – was 'Resurrection Bob' alias Brixham smuggler Bob Elliott. He used to store contraband in a large cave in the cliffs of Berry Head. When this was full on one occasion, a cargo of brandy kegs had to be stored in his own cottage. Customs officers were tipped-off and went to the cottage only to be told Bob had died during the night. The respectful officers decided it would be insensitive to search the premises and so retired empty-handed. On the following day a large coffin arrived at the cottage – the perfect size to transport some kegs of brandy! During the night coastguards spotted a procession of men carrying the coffin – one of which was Bob Elliott! The superstitious coastguards, believing they had seen a ghostly vision, fled in terror. The truth soon became apparent, but officers did not take any action as they were too embarrassed to reveal to the public how easily they had been duped.

The poor customs officers were always up against it, not only because of the smugglers' cunningness, but because most of the villagers were in league with the traders. At one stage, officers were not employed within 20 miles of their home as it was almost certain they would know friends involved in the trade!

Devon had a reputation for smuggling, but never on a scale as great as the South East counties which were in easy reach of the capital to market goods. Towards the end of the 19th century the trade began to die down, though of course smuggling still exists even today. It is however unlikely the modern-day smuggler will ever earn the immortal fame of his predecessors.

Wrecking

Murder on the coast of Devon

While smugglers often became heroes, the coast's notorious wreckers became the scourge of society. Shining their lights to lure ships onto rocks in the pretence of guiding them through the storm was just the beginning of their callous actions. Once the ship had been wrecked they would work frantically to save the valuable cargo, ignoring the blood-curdling cries of the dying seamen. As an old saying went:

'Save a stranger from the sea
And he'll prove your enemy.'

They knew dead men told no tales and so any 'lucky' survivors were normally brutally finished off.

The term wreckers is a broad one as most 'wreckers' were simply scavengers and played no part in the actual wrecking of the ship. They consisted of ordinary villagers hoping to cash in on the misfortune of others. The demise of a ship was a godsend for many people as it gave them a chance to relieve their poverty-stricken lives with a little luxury.

Just like smuggling, all types of the community were involved and at times a whole village would attempt to benefit. During one stormy Sunday morning, a priest giving a sermon at East Portlemouth Church, was interrupted by a man who rushed in red-faced to announce a ship had gone down at Prawle Point. The priest wasted no time in tearing off his vestments and, with his congregation hot on his heels, hurried down to the shore to witness the last few moments of the sinking Spanish galleon. The villagers had not come to help the dying seamen however, and only had eyes for the precious cargo, despite the imploring pleas of the mariners. All the crew were lost and it is said their terrifying screams can still be heard on a wet and stormy morning.

The problem of ships being looted by ordinary people became so bad wreck guards were appointed to stop villagers running away with the vessel's cargo. Unfortunately, most guards were easily bribed or were tempted to take a share of the goods themselves. In 1860, a wreck guard was found dead beside the wreck of the Prussian barque Frederick II which had come ashore off Hartland Point. He is believed to have fallen unconscious and died of exposure after helping himself to the ship's liquor!

Wreck guards could do very little to stop wreckers as they were often outnumbered and threatened by groups of up to about 20 men. The enormity of their task is highlighted by the tale of the warship *La Carpe*, which was wrecked at Abbotsham Cliffs in 1750. More than 2,000 people are believed to have descended on the wreck in order to help themselves, fighting each other like madmen to get the best of the booty. The looters also helped themselves to the ship's wine and had no trouble getting through the 250 gallons believed to have been on board!

The authorities had to act quickly to thwart the wreckers once a ship had gone down. Within an hour of the *Princess Royal* being forced ashore at Baggy Point in 1848, her valuable £20,000 cargo was being landed by coastguards. The furious wreckers who had arrived in droves for a share of the spoils vented their anger by throwing rocks at the salvage men.

While the south coast of Devon became the home of smuggling, the north coast became the home of wrecking. The unpredictable Atlantic Ocean and one of the most treacherous coastlines in the country provided an ideal hunting ground for wreckers.

The most famous wrecker who inhabited this area was 'Cruel' Coppinger, who plied his trade on the hazardous shores around Hartland. Coppinger was believed to have been a Danish sea captain shipwrecked at Welcombe Mouth at the end of the 18th century. Perhaps his misfortune gave him the idea for his own reign of terror, for he too was at the mercy of wreckers when his ship was grounded. News had filtered through that a ship had been wrecked off the coast and so a group of villagers had raced to the scene to 'greet' it. Wreckers were already common along this part of the coast and Coppinger knew it. As the only survivor he realised he would be silenced and so hid until an opportune moment to escape came his way. As the villagers fought for the cargo, Coppinger fled past them and made his escape on one of their horses. The horse naturally carried Coppinger to its home where he was given shelter by a compassionate farmer, and within a year he had married the farmer's daughter, Dinah Hamlyn, at Hartland Church.

For the next few years Coppinger began to earn his 'cruel' nickname, mercilessly going about his sordid business on the north coast. Smuggling, wrecking and attacking any kind of ship in his own vessel known as The Black Prince were just some of his favourite pastimes.

Another hobby was to ill-treat his wife and he frequently stole money from Dinah and her family. Coppinger was continually harassed by customs officers, but always escaped them. On one occasion he beheaded an exciseman on the gunwale of his boat.

If Coppinger's arrival was dramatic, his departure was equally exciting. With customs officers closing in on him all the time, Coppinger decided to make his escape. Nobody knew anything about his plan but he was spotted one night on top of Gull Rock near Marshland Mouth signalling to a ship. The vessel was seen to pick him up and take him away. According to legend a fierce storm broke at the precise moment they left the shore. It is believed the boat was overturned in the gale and wrecked. Coppinger drowned – and locals would have told you the ghosts of his many wreck victims had finally gained their revenge!

There are so many different variations on the legend of Coppinger it is difficult to know what the truth really is. Records show a Daniel Coppinger married a Anne Hamlyn at Hartland Parish Church in 1793, but many say this was not 'Cruel' Coppinger. Some people even go as far as to say the whole story was made up by local smugglers to keep frightened people away from the caves where they operated.

Evidence of Coppinger and other professional wreckers deliberately luring ships to their destruction is scarce. In fact, there have been very few prosecutions for actual wrecking. This, of course, does not mean professional wrecking did not occur. Proof a ship had been deliberately lured onto cliffs was difficult to obtain. All the wreckers needed to operate was a signalman on a hill with a lantern. Few survivors could testify they had been guided by a light on the cliffs because there were rarely any survivors – the wreckers would see to that!

The modern-day wreckers are certainly not as cruel as Coppinger, but have still proved to be a nuisance to the authorities. Mindless vandalism and hundreds of curious sightseers wishing to take back a special souvenir have caused major problems. In 1982, national newspapers claimed about 200 'wreckers' descended on the usually remote Hartland Point during a Bank Holiday weekend. They had arrived to see the 960-tonne Panamanian vessel Johanna, which had come ashore hundreds of yards from the Point. Within a few days the ship had virtually been stripped.

Legends and Strange Tales

Unusual stories conceived on Devon's coast

The coast of Devon is home to more than a few strange legends and tales. While many were based on fact, many also appear to have no foundation whatsoever and were more likely created from the minds of imaginative storytellers. A number are recorded below, though I will leave it up to you to judge their authenticity!

Sir Francis Drake

There are more stories and tales surrounding Sir Francis Drake than any other Devonian, or even Englishman come to that! Drake was a living legend and some locals believed he was capable of anything. Before tackling the Spanish Armada in 1588 he is said to have asked for a hatchet and some timber where upon he began chopping up the wood to throw into Plymouth Sound. As the wood hit the water, the timber ignited and formed a fireship which went on to defeat the Spaniards.

As well as fighting for his country, Drake was also responsible for ending a severe drought in Plymouth. It is said the great seafarer went to Dartmoor and ordered a stream to follow him. It obeyed and he rode into the city to bring a much-needed water supply to the stricken Plymouth people.

The popular seaman also warned the country of imminent war – or at least his drum did! Drake's Drum, which is now on show at his former home at Buckland Abbey, was said to beat on its own accord whenever the country was threatened by enemy attack.

Living legend Sir Francis Drake stands proudly on Plymouth Hoe.

Even after his death, Drake was believed to be hard at work for the country. Before he died, he told his adoring public he would return – and he did, according to many, in the guise of Lord Nelson!

Of course there is one tale always associated with Drake. Did he really decide to finish his game of bowls on the Hoe before giving his attention to the advancing Spaniards? The answer is probably yes – though his coolness has now been attributed to the fact he knew he would have been unable to set sail right away as he had to wait for the right tide!

The Rector of South Pool

Sitting half-way up the Kingsbridge estuary is the tiny village of South Pool with its splendid church of St Nicholas. The rector there during the mid-17th century was the Rev William Streat. He was not your average man of the cloth, however, for he blessed his forthcoming marriage with a local girl by getting her pregnant!

When the girl's family discovered there was to be an addition to the household, they were furious and demanded the rector did the decent thing and marry their daughter immediately. The only snag was the rector had died a few weeks earlier! Not that this bothered the family, for they preceded to dig up his body and perform the marriage ceremony themselves!

What happened during the honeymoon one can only guess, but the rector was not re-laid to rest until 1668 – some two years later!

Daddy's Hole

At Daddyhole Plain on the cliffs of Torquay close to Meadfoot Beach is a deep cleft in the rocks known as Daddy's or Devil's Hole. According to legend it was the scene of a bitter tale of love and revenge which came to a dramatic and tragic conclusion.

It all began when a beautiful maiden fell in love with a knight long ago. Unfortunately he did not share the same feelings for her and pledged his love to another. Despite the maiden's desperate attempts to win him, the knight stayed loyal to his own sweet-heart.

The unhappy maiden soon gave up all hope and took to wandering along the lonely seashore thinking about her rival with a bitter and jealous heart. One night, as she walked along the shore, she began to hear the haunting cries of baying hounds. As the terrible monster-like creatures came into view, the maiden fainted – for leading them on horseback was the Devil himself.

When the maiden came round all was quiet and a handsome young man was leaning over her. After assuring her there was no demon huntsman anywhere in sight they began to talk and before long the maiden had opened her heart to the caring stranger. Touched by her tragic story, the man promised her revenge on the knight and his sweetheart, so long as the maiden in return pledged her love for him for ever. Such was the hatred towards her rival, the maiden agreed and the stranger went off to find the couple. On his return he informed her they could be found under the moon on the shore, now know as Daddy's Hole. Without haste the maiden went to the spot, and while the two lovers held each other in their arms, crept up unnoticed and stabbed them with a dagger. As they died a fierce storm broke and through the crack-ing thunder, the maiden once again heard the howls of the baying hounds. In the middle of the pack was the demon huntsman, spurring them on with a whip. As he got closer a flash of lightning illuminated his face and the horrified maiden saw it was none other than her handsome stranger!

Her attempts to flee were in vain and she was soon caught by the vicious hounds of Hell. The Devil reminded the maiden of her promise and roared triumphantly she belonged to him for-ever. With one swift movement he swept her into his arms and rode into the rocks which opened up before him. The maiden was never seen again, though the hole in the cliff-face can still be seen today.

The Parson and the Clerk

A permanent reminder of an ambitious parson and his clerk can be seen in the form of two rocks at Holcombe between Teignmouth and Dawlish. The parson longed to become the Bishop of Exeter and was said to stop at nothing to achieve his goal. He had been promised the post when it became vacant and so when news broke that the present bishop was dying, the excited parson decided to pay him a personal visit to make sure the rumours were true.

A sinister story lies behind The Parson and Clerk headland at Holcombe.

On the way to the bishop's home in Dawlish, a terrific storm erupted and the parson and his clerk soon became hopelessly lost. The frustrated parson blamed his clerk and said he would rather have the Devil as a guide. No sooner had he uttered his careless remark, a stranger appeared and invited them to his mansion until the storm subsided. The two guests were treated to a hearty meal and a drink or two to celebrate the parson's imminent promotion.

More than a little tipsy, they bade farewell a little later and prepared to mount their horses. When the horses refused to budge, the angry parson cried out in anger: 'The Devil take them!' Their host smiled and replied: 'Thank you. I will.' With that the horses galloped into the sea taking with them their two riders. The following morning, locals woke to find two new rocks attached to the headland – the parson and his clerk.

The Devil's Footprints

On a winter's night in 1855 the villages and towns of the Exe Estuary received an unobserved visitor who was to leave his mark in the area for ever.

The people of Exmouth, Lympstone, Topsham, on the east side and Starcross, Dawlish and Teignmouth, on the west, woke up one morning to discover hundreds of footprints in the snow. Nothing unusual you may think, but all the newly-made prints had been made by what looked like the hooves of a donkey. Another problem was the creature appeared to have only two legs!

Locals in Lympstone, where footprints were found all over the town including up walls and on roofs, were convinced they had been made by the Devil and refused to leave their homes the following night.

The strange incident gained national media coverage. Animal experts said it would have been almost impossible for an animal to cover such a wide area in one night or to have swam across the estuary. To this day no explanation has ever been found and the footprints remain a mystery.

The Blank Monk of Lynton

It is not difficult to understand why so many legends are associated with the mysterious and inspiring Valley of the Rocks at Lynton.

The most famous concerns a knight who is said to have ruled in a castle on the edge of the once green and lush valley. One stormy evening, while he was away, a man dressed in the dark habit of a monk knocked on the huge castle door and demanded some assistance. The knight's suspicious wife mistrusted the visitor's dark and gloomy appearance and refused him entry. With this the angry monk clenched his fist and cursed the knight and his family.

'All that is thine shall be mine, until in the porch of the holy church a lady and a child shall stand and beckon,' he raged.

Many years passed and the greedy knight, ignoring the monk's eerie warning, decided to demolish a local church in order to use its treasures to enhance his own castle. It was not long before the Black Monk appeared before him – and by the following morning the knight was found dead, slumped across his treasure chest.

With the strange curse still ringing in the ears of the petrified family, the knight's son left his mother and younger sister to make amends by joining the Crusaders in the Holy Land. During the many battles he fought he was said to have been accompanied by a blank monk who never left his side and encouraged him to lead a wild life. His mother and sister, on learning of his wicked ways, died soon after, broken-hearted because their beloved son had turned against God. When he heard about their deaths, the son returned to Devon filled with remorse and headed to the church to repent. The evil Black Monk, holding his hand tightly, urged him not to go and did everything to stop him, but the tearful young knight, believing he could see his mother and younger sister in the church porch, resisted the monk and walked towards them praying for forgiveness. As he reached them he was embraced and the three were taken up to Heaven. A roll of thunder split the earth open as they departed and the furious Black Monk leapt into the abyss. The earth closed up around him and the towers of the castle began to crumble until the enormous fortress crashed to the ground. The fragments of its stone walls were scattered across the valley and remain in the spot they fell to this day. The largest of which is now known as Castle Rock.

Jennifred's Leap

Close to Duty Point Tower in Lee Bay near Lynton is a crag known as Jennifred's Leap. It got its name from Jennifred de Whichehalse who lived at Ley Manor (now Lee Abbey) during the reign of James II. She is said to have given her heart to Lord Auberley – one of the King's most loyal supporters. Unfortunately he did not share the same feelings and cruelly broke off the relationship. The devastated Jennifred could no longer go on living and so took herself to the cliff and leapt into the sea to her death. Her distraught father went to the King to vent his anger in the hope Auberley would be punished, but nothing was done. Vowing he would avenge his daughter's death, de Whichehalse turned against the King and joined the Duke of Monmouth's rebels.

The chance to take his revenge did not take long in coming for de Whichehalse was said to have met and killed Auberley on the battlefield at Sedgemoor.

The Red Petticoats of Ilfracombe

It took a lot of courage and plenty of cannon balls to suppress 18th-century French sea attacks – though in Ilfracombe the humblest of womens' under-garments proved just as successful!

It was in 1797 the town's modest women were prompted to reveal their secret weapons. Four French ships had been sighted off the coast and the town feared for the worst as most of Ilfracombe's sailors were away. The ingenious women of Ilfracombe wasted no time in climbing to the highest points of the town where they proceeded to remove their traditional red petti-coats and place them over their shoulders like cloaks.

Whether indeed the French were fooled into thinking the town had a strong military force lining up to meet them it will never be known – but the four ships sailed away and were never seen again.

The Braunds of Bucks

Look through gravestones in villages all over the country and in each place you will find at least one name which is prominent throughout the centuries. The tiny sloping village of Bucks Mills on the North Devon coast is no exception. The name Braund will be familiar with almost every resident.

During the 19th century the entire village was almost com-pletely made up of Braunds. Where they originated from remains a mystery, for they were unlike the ordinary Devonshire folk in appearance, being dark-skinned and of thin build. According to legend they were the descendents of shipwrecked Spaniards from the Armada. It is said they came ashore at Bucks Mills and settled as fishermen, marrying the local girls and gradually taking over the whole village – some say by force.

Whatever their origin, there is no doubting their bravery to-wards those who found themselves in trouble at sea. The Braunds operated their own coastal rescue service for many years using their own boats. The most famous was Captain James Braund who was known as the King of Bucks and lived in the cliff-top King's Cottage with his wife and ten children. He was an expert sailor and pilot over the notorious Bideford bar for more than 40 years, during which time he boasted he never lost a vessel or a life.

His bravery was highlighted in 1850 when he spotted the American vessel *Grace Darling* in trouble out at sea during atrocious conditions. When the rescue boat from Clovelly was forced to turn back, he and his brother launched their own small herring boat and battled to reach the struggling vessel through enormous breakers, described by locals as the size of mountains. The *Grace Darling* somehow managed to reach Appledore with the captain's boat following, but the latter was struggling to stay afloat. Witnesses from a hill at Appledore watched in horror, resigned to the fact it would only be a matter of time before the boat and the two men were lost for ever. But incredibly they made it safely into port nearly three hours after launching their rescue boat. They were greeted as heroes and many described it as the most skilled display of piloting ever witnessed. Some even went as far as to say the amazing Captain Braund had control over the sea itself.

In 1873, a small book was produced to honour Captain Braund and included descriptions of his amazing rescues. Gradually, the Braunds moved away from Bucks Mills and today descendants can be found throughout the world. In 1932, the Braund Society was founded and it is still thriving today – even though there is believed to be only one Braund left in the village itself.

Mystery may surround their origin, but there is no doubting the Braunds left their mark in the beautiful village of Bucks Mills.

The Cannibals of Clovelly

From the tiny, peaceful village of Clovelly comes a savage tale which you might find a little difficult to swallow! Very few now believe the Cannibals of Clovelly even existed and many think the whole incredible story was made up by smugglers in a bid to keep people away from the caves where they stored their contraband. I will leave it up to you to digest the facts and decide for yourself!

John Gregg and his wife lived with their eight sons, six daughters and 32 grandchildren in a cave at Clovelly for at least 25 years during the 18th century. Perhaps because there were so many mouths to feed, the family declined visiting the local supermarket choosing instead to feed upon travellers! It is said about 1,000 people were murdered and eaten by the Gregg family. Certainly, to keep up their hermit-like existence for so long they would have needed a large supply of meat from somewhere. Suspicions only arose people were being murdered when it was discovered the already sparse North Devon population seemed to be dwindling further!

A group of about 400 men – such was the Gregg's fearful reputation – was assembled to put a stop to their dastardly deeds. Armed with bloodhounds they found the family's cave and discovered it to be full of bones and dried bodies hanging like meat in a butcher's shop. The Greggs were taken to Plymouth and executed without trial. It is believed they showed little remorse. Because they were not considered to be human they did not receive any kind of burial and their ashes were left to blow away in the wind.

Index of Place Names

We publish guides to individual towns, plus books on walking and cycling in the great outdoors throughout England and Wales. This is a recent selection:

More Books about the South-West

MYTHS AND LEGENDS OF CORNWALL – Craig Weatherhill & Paul Devereux *(£6.95)*

CORNISH PLACE NAMES & LANGUAGE – Craig Weatherhill *(£6.95)*

BEST PUB WALKS IN NORTH DEVON – Dennis Needham *(£6.95(*

PUB WALKS IN SOUTH DEVON – Laurence Main *(£6.95)*

PUB WALKS ON DARTMOOR – Laurence Main *(£6.95)*

PUB WALKS IN CORNWALL – Laurebce Main *(£6.95)*

PUB WALKS ON EXMOOR – Philip Pond *(£6.95)*

CYCLING IN THE WEST COUNTRY – Helen Stephenson *(£7.95)*

Other Destinations

FIFTY CLASSIC WALKS IN THE PENNINES – Terry Marsh *(£8.95)*

HILL WALKS IN MID WALES – Dave Ing *(£8.95)*

WEST PENNINE WALKS – Mike Cresswell *(£5.95)*

WELSH WALKS: Dolgellau /Cambrian Coast – L. Main & M. Perrott *(£5.95)*

WELSH WALKS: Aberystwyth & District – L. Main & M. Perrott *(£5.95)*

WALKS IN MYSTERIOUS WALES – Laurence Main *(£7.95)*

RAMBLES IN NORTH WALES – Roger Redfern *(£6.95)*

RAMBLES AROUND MANCHESTER – Mike Cresswell *(£5.95)*

EAST CHESHIRE WALKS – Graham Beech *(£5.95)*

CHALLENGING WALKS: NW England & N Wales – Ron Astley *(£7.95)*

LONDON BUS-TOP TOURIST – John Wittich *(£6.95)*

TEA SHOP WALKS IN THE CHILTERNS – Jean Patefield *(£6.95)*

BY-WAY TRAVELS SOUTH OF LONDON – Geoff Marshall *(£6.95)*

BY-WAY BIKING IN THE CHILTERNS – Henry Tindell *(£7.95)*

PUB WALKS IN SNOWDONIA – Laurence Main *(£6.95)*

BEST PUB WALKS AROUND CHESTER & THE DEE VALLEY – John Haywood *(£6.95)*

BEST PUB WALKS IN GWENT – Les Lumsdon *(£6.95)*

PUB WALKS IN POWYS – Les Lumsdon & Chris Rushton *(£6.95)*

BEST PUB WALKS IN PEMBROKESHIRE – Laurence Main *(£6.95)*

BEST PUB WALKS AROUND CENTRAL LONDON – Ruth Herman *(£6.95)*

BEST PUB WALKS IN ESSEX – Derek Keeble *(£6.95)*

More Pub Walks . . .

There are many more titles in our fabulous series of 'Pub Walks' books for just about every popular walking area in the UK, all featuring access by public transport. We label our more recent ones as 'best' to differentiate them from inferior competitors!

Explore the Lake District:

THE LAKELAND SUMMITS – Tim Synge *(£7.95)*

100 LAKE DISTRICT HILL WALKS – Gordon Brown *(£7.95)*

LAKELAND ROCKY RAMBLES: Geology beneath your feet – Brian Lynas *(£7.95)*

FULL DAYS ON THE LAKELAND FELLS: Challenging Walks – Adrian Dixon *(£7.95)*

PUB WALKS IN THE LAKE DISTRICT – Neil Coates *(£6.95)*

LAKELAND WALKING, ON THE LEVEL – Norman Buckley *(£6.95)*

MOSTLY DOWNHILL: LEISURELY WALKS, LAKE DISTRICT – Alan Pears *(£6.95)*

Cycling . . .

CYCLE UK! The essential guide to leisure cycling – Les Lumsdon *(£9.95)*

OFF-BEAT CYCLING IN THE PEAK DISTRICT – Clive Smith *(£6.95)*

MORE OFF-BEAT CYCLING IN THE PEAK DISTRICT – Clive Smith *(£6.95)*

50 BEST CYCLE RIDES IN CHESHIRE – edited by Graham Beech *(£7.95)*

CYCLING IN THE COTSWOLDS – Stephen Hill *(£6.95)*

CYCLING IN THE CHILTERNS – Henry Tindell *(£7.95)*

CYCLING IN THE LAKE DISTRICT – John Wood *(£7.95)*

CYCLING IN LINCOLNSHIRE – Penny & Bill Howe *(£7.95)*

CYCLING IN NOTTINGHAMSHIRE – Penny & Bill Howe *(£7.95)*

CYCLING IN STAFFORDSHIRE – Linda Wain *(£7.95)*

CYCLING IN THE WEST COUNTRY – Helen Stephenson *(£7.95)*

CYCLING IN SOUTH WALES – Rosemary Evans *(£7.95)*

CYCLING IN NORTH WALES – Philip Routledge *(£7.95)* ... *available 1996*

Sport . . .

RED FEVER: from Rochdale to Rio as 'United' supporters – Steve Donoghue *(£7.95)*

UNITED WE STOOD: unofficial history of the Ferguson years – Richard Kurt *(£6.95)*

MANCHESTER CITY: Moments to Remember – John Creighton *(£9.95)*

- plus many more entertaining and educational books being regularly added to our list. All of our books are available from your local bookshop. In case of difficulty, or to obtain our complete catalogue, please contact:

Sigma Leisure, 1 South Oak Lane, Wilmslow, Cheshire SK9 6AR
Phone: 01625 – 531035   Fax: 01625 – 536800

ACCESS and VISA orders welcome – call our friendly sales staff or use our 24 hour Answerphone service! Most orders are despatched on the day we receive your order – you could be enjoying our books in just a couple of days. Please add £2 p&p to all orders.